# Brigham Young

## The New York Years

Charles
Redd
Monographs
in Western
History No. 14

The
New York
Years

# Brigham Young

Richard F. Palmer and Karl D. Butler

Charles Redd Center for Western Studies

*The Charles Redd Monographs in Western History are made possible by a grant from Charles Redd. This grant served as the basis for the establishment of the Charles Redd Center for Western Studies at Brigham Young University.*

*Center editors: Thomas G. Alexander*
*Howard A. Christy*

ISBN    0-941214-07-9

Charles Redd Center for Western Studies

Distributed by Signature Books, Midvale, Utah

# Contents

65491

# Preface

Brigham Young died a little more than a century ago, but he is remembered today as one of the most controversial and legendary personalities in American history—a dynamic religious leader and hearty pioneer who led the Mormons to the Great Basin in 1847. As a colonizer, he displayed remarkable leadership and business ability and was largely responsible for the settling of the vast Intermountain West stretching from Canada southward into the heart of Mexico. In addition to being instrumental in establishing numerous communities, he pioneered in the construction of railroads, highways, telegraph lines, irrigation systems, churches, and tabernacles. And he established forts, factories, mines, banks, and stores.

What many do not know is that Brigham Young prepared for his life's mission in the state of New York. He was born in Vermont, taken to New York State as an infant, and raised on hard work by deeply religious parents. He lived and worked during most of his first thirty years in the heart of the Finger Lakes region.

A willing worker, but lacking formal education, Brigham learned and practiced a variety of trades. At the age of sixteen he was apprenticed to a furniture and cabinet maker in Auburn. Young Brigham became, in time, an expert husbandman, farmer, gardener, carpenter, glazier, mason, furniture and cabinet maker, painter, and boat builder—and even took a turn at lay preaching.

Many of Brigham's closest associates in later life, we discovered, were old friends whom he had first met in New York State. Perhaps the most noted of these was his close confidant Heber C. Kimball, who also came from Vermont parentage. And there was Solomon Chamberlain, with whom

Brigham later crossed the Plains. Chamberlain was to become one of the first members of the Mormon church and appears to have been the first unofficial missionary to make direct contact with the Young family.

Inspired by the late Mrs. Mary Van Sickle Wait of Auburn, this work has been carefully researched and chronicled, employing every available resource. Mrs. Wait and her husband, H. R. Wait, for many years spent their summers at a beautiful country home just west of Auburn. They had been told by the former owner that Brigham Young, as a youth, "had something to do with the construction of the house." In her later years, wishing to do something worthwhile as a legacy to her community, Mrs. Wait set out to gather materials relating to Brigham Young's early life in Cayuga County. Eventually she published a small monograph, *Brigham Young in Cayuga County* (Ithaca, N. Y.: DeWitt Historical Society, 1964).

Before Mrs. Wait's death in 1973 (and her husband's subsequent death in 1975), we were given permission to reprint the earlier work or to revise it based on new findings. The Waits expressed the hope that their work, together with any additional pertinent material, would receive wider distribution than had the initial publication.

Our original intent was simply to reprint the Wait booklet, adding pertinent corrections and refinements. After a period of exhaustive research, however, we determined that the significant amount of "new" material would require a completely revised work. In addition, much of Mrs. Wait's research needed documentation. Even now, although every known avenue has been pursued for additional facts, our own monograph is likely not definitive.

We express our appreciation to the following individuals and organizations for their assistance during research for this monograph. First, we thank Ronald Esplin, research historian with the Historical Department of The Church of Jesus Christ of Latter-day Saints, who pointed out correspondence by Brigham Young referring to his early life. Second, we thank members of the John Young Family Association, who furnished genealogical material on the Young family not readily available elsewhere. Institutions generous with their resources were Brigham Young University, Provo, Utah; Cayuga County Historian's Office, Auburn, New York; Chenango County Historical Society, Norwich, New York; American Baptist Historical Society, Rochester, New York; Ontario County Historical Society, Canandaigua, New York; Cornell University's Department of Regional History; and DeWitt Historical Society of Tompkins County, Ithaca, New York, publishers of the initial monograph.

Individuals offering assistance and encouragement included Professor Larry C. Porter, Brigham Young University; J. Sheldon Fisher, Fisher's, New York, who has spent many years collecting material relating to the Mormons in Mendon, New York; Mrs. Vaughan Fargo, historian of Smyrna, New York; Mrs. Diane C. Ham, Honeoye Falls, New York, historian of Mendon; Mrs. Kenneth Coulson, Scipio Center, New York, historian and genealogist; Karl Kabelach, Rush Rhees Library, University of Rochester; Lewis L. Parker, Ogden, Utah; and Ralph Webster, Auburn, New York.

In preparing the monograph for publication we were assisted by Professor Leonard J. Arrington, Brigham Young University, and JoAnn Jolley, assistant editor, The Ensign, monthly magazine of The Church of Jesus Christ of Latter-day Saints, published in Salt Lake City.

Richard F. Palmer<br>Karl D. Butler

## CHAPTER ONE

# The John Young Family
# 1801-1817

*"My Father was a poor, honest, hard-working man . . . and his mind seemingly stretched from east to west, from north to south; and to the day of his death he wanted to command worlds; but the Lord would never permit him to get rich."*
Brigham Young
Sermon of January 5, 1860
*Journal of Discourses*, 10: 360

Breaking family ties, pulling up stakes, and venturing into the uncharted wilderness characterized the American pioneer spirit following the Revolutionary War. Until that time, most of the nation's population had been concentrated on the Eastern Seaboard, particularly in the middle Atlantic states. John Young, Brigham Young's father and a veteran of the Revolution, was a product of this restless generation.[1] He was short and stocky, if his son Lorenzo's description of him as being five feet, eight inches tall and weighing about 165 pounds is accurate. According to Lorenzo,

> he had light hair, and blue eyes. He had a small mouth and thin lips denoting considerable firmness of character. He was strong and active; very few men of his size being able to perform the same amount of labor.
> He lived in the days when they cut hay with a hand scythe. I can remember him as the best mower in the section where he lived. After he was fifty years old I

remember a young man saying: "Uncle John Young is the best mower in this town."[2]

Brigham described his father as strict, devout, and rather dour—a man who would have easily fit the image said to be typical of eighteenth-century New Englanders of Puritan extraction. Said Brigham, "My father . . . was very circumspect, exemplary and religious. . . ."[3] As a disciplinarian, Brigham stated that "it used to be a word and a blow, with him, and the blow came first."[4] Still, Brigham's perceptions aside, his brother Lorenzo claimed that Brigham was "a favorite of father's, who I never knew to find fault with him but once."[5]

John's restlessness, as well as financial need, resulted in a number of moves, the first apparently occurring in the period 1788-89, and the second in 1801, the year of Brigham Young's birth. From Hopkinton, Massachusetts, where John had met and married his first wife, Abigail (Nabby), the family, which at the time already numbered eight children, moved about eighty miles northwest to Whitingham, Windham County, in southern Vermont.[6] There John purchased fifty acres of farm land (for fifty dollars) from his wealthy brother-in-law, Joseph Mosely.[7]

Apparently unsuccessful at his Vermont farming enterprise, John sold the land back to his brother-in-law in late 1802, packed up his family, and moved to what was to become the town of Smyrna, Chenango County, New York, a distance of almost 130 miles, "where he followed farming, clearing new land, and enduring many privations and hardships with his family, incidental to new settlements."[8] Brigham's older brother Joseph recalled that "the town of Sherburn [sic] was divided and one part called Smyrna, and here my brother Lorenzo was born, in the same place as sister Louisa, but different name. Here my sister Nabby died in 1807 and the same year we moved to Cold Brook where we lived five years."[9]

Joseph Young's account concurs with local tradition that the Youngs lived near Cold Brook in a rural neighborhood called "Dark Hollow," about three miles southwest of the village of Smyrna.[10] It is believed that their home was a log dwelling on the west side of a road leading from "Dark Hollow" to nearby "German Hollow."[11]

In those days, every able-bodied man in the community was required to work on public roads and highways for a specified number of days each year. John Young's name appears on the highway assessment list of Sherburne, 8th and 9th townships, District 21, for two days' work in 1808. District 21 was defined as "beginning at the School House near Obediah Harrington's; thence southwestwardly by Wm. Stover's to the town line including the road by Ebenezer Baker's, also a road to John Brown's."[12] John Young's name also appears in the 1810 Federal Census of Smyrna, Chenango County. Family records indicate that the household at this time included John, his wife, Abigail, sons Brigham, Lorenzo Dow, Phinehas, and Joseph, and daughters Louisa, Susannah, Rhoda, and Fanny.

Family moves continued to be a part of the John Young family's life. Joseph recorded that "in the winter of 1813 my father moved his family to the town of Genoa [fifty miles west of Smyrna] in the county of Cayuga, on the shore of the lake of the same name." The exact location of the Young home in that vicinity cannot be determined from the sparse evidence available. Quite possibly the Youngs lived about seven miles southwest of Genoa, near Lansing or Lansingville. (Unfortunately, no deeds have been located to indicate that John Young purchased property in either Cayuga or Tomkins counties.) Residence at or near Lansingville (North Lansing) is indicated by the fact that Abigail was buried near there—and that Lansingville, not Genoa, was located on the shore of Cayuga Lake (Genoa was then and still is about seven miles east of the lake).[13]

Abigail faithfully stood by her husband throughout their marriage although for many years she was afflicted with consumption (tuberculosis), a common illness in pioneer times—in Abigail's case an illness made more protracted by the repeated pregnancies, the several moves, and the lack of doctors generally in that part of the frontier.

In her younger days, Abigail had been a beautiful woman with blue eyes and ash blond hair which waved gracefully across her brow. She and her sisters had been accomplished singers, popular at social gatherings back in Hopkinton, where they had enlivened the air with old English madrigals. It is said that Brigham inherited his large frame and dignified appearance from his mother's side of the family.[14] Lorenzo Dow remembered their mother as a praying, fervent woman. "She frequently called me to her bedside and counseled me to be a good man that the Lord might bless my life. On one occasion she told me that if I would not neglect to pray to my Heavenly Father, he would send a guardian angel to protect me in the dangers to which I might be exposed."[15]

Abigail died on June 11, 1815. Several historical accounts indicate that she was buried near Lansingville, possibly in the old White Settlement Cemetery, a half mile west of that village.[16]

Apparently young Brigham deeply loved and respected his mother, and was much influenced by her.

> Of my mother—she that bore me—I can say, no better woman ever lived in the world than she was. I have the feelings of a son towards her: I should have them—it is right; but I judge the matter pertaining to her from the principles and the spirit of the teachings I received from her.
>
> Would she countenance one of her children in the least act that was wrong according to her traditions? No, not in the least degree.[17]

Dr. J. P. Barnum is reported to have said of that relationship:

> Having left the country soon after the death of his mother, he became a wanderer and adventurer; but during his mother's life he was remembered as a very studious, industrious boy, and very much devoted to his mother. The family being very poor, he devoted most of his time to hunting and fishing for their support. One of his chief characteristics was his great taciturnity. He held himself aloof from the boys of his own age, and seemed to care for nothing but study and to work for his mother.[18]

4

Nancy, Susannah, Rhoda, and Fanny had married and moved away by 1815. As Nabby had died previously (in 1807), of the five daughters only Louisa, aged eleven, remained with the family. However, Fanny left her husband, Robert Carr, who had been unfaithful, returned home, and took over care of the family shortly before Abigail's death.[19]

Soon after Abigail's death, John Young again moved westward, to the "Sugar Hill" district of Steuben (now Schuyler) County, near Tyrone, some thirty-five miles from Genoa.[20] Apparently, he took with him only Joseph, Brigham, and Phinehas—and probably Fanny. John, Jr. married (at the age of twenty-two) Theodocia Kimball in 1813. Lorenzo went to live with his older sister Rhoda, the wife of John P. Greene (since 1813), an itinerant Methodist preacher, near Cayuga Bridge (Cayuga). Louisa most likely also went to live with the Greenes—or, at least temporarily, with sister Susannah, the wife of James Little (since 1814), in the vicinity of nearby Auburn.[21]

John Young and his family experienced a wearisome trek through the forests before they reached their new home. Lorenzo wrote that his father "moved to what was then considered the Far West," where the family settled in the midst of a dense wilderness "of about 20 miles in length and breadth." Here John purchased one hundred acres from a General Wordsworth, "on what was then called 'Wordsworth Tract,' which had just been opened for market."[22] The Young home was situated "in a dense forest fifteen miles from any settlement where there were any supplies to be gotten."[23]

According to local sources, the family settled on a farm near Pine Grove, seven miles west of what is now Watkins Glen, on Sugar Hill Road.[24] A "portion" of the Young family are said to have lived for a time on the premises later occupied by "Uncle Dan" Hughey, about a half-mile south of Pine Grove.[25]

Jabez Hamner, an early settler who arrived in 1815 with his family, "stored his goods, and lived in the house of John Young, until he could build for himself. When Mr. Hamner came, John Young and his family and Daniel Kent were the only settlers in this part of the town."[26]

The John Young family was soon joined (in the fall of 1815) by Rhoda and John Greene who brought Lorenzo with them. The whereabouts of Fanny and Louisa at that time is uncertain. That they were not with the family in the fall of 1815 is indicated by James A. Little, Lorenzo's biographer, who stated that there were no female members with the family from late 1815 through 1816.[27]

Some time after the family's arrival in the Sugar Hill district, John married Hannah Dennis Brown, a widow with several children of her own. Sources vary widely as to the date of that union. Hannah claimed it was 1815, family records set the date as 1816, and Brigham recalled the date to be 1817.[28] (A marriage date of 1816 or 1817 is the most plausible.) Three children were born to John and Hannah. Two died in infancy and the third, Edward, was born July 30, 1823.[29]

For generations the Sugar Hill district had been known for its fine groves of maple trees. John Young, wrote Lorenzo, "had a nice lot of sugar maples on his place. He made troughs and tapped the sugar bush."[30] Farmers always looked forward to "sugaring-off" season in the early spring; it was a harvest as important as haying and corn husking. Not only did maple sugar have household uses, but it was used as barter to purchase essential items.

Working on the farm, Brigham hauled maple sap, and when his father had made fifty or sixty pounds of sugar, Brigham put it on his back and started for the settlement to exchange it for flour, "as all our flour was gone and that was our main living, in those days. Our boys would think it hard fare to sit down to a breakfast of nothing but bread, water and porridge, although that was our living, only as my brother John would once in awhile kill a deer or perhaps a partridge."[31]

Brigham's oldest brother, John, Jr., was an expert marksman and was fond of the chase.[32] But on one occasion John was not around to bring home a deer for supper. Lorenzo related the incident.

On this occasion father had been gone two days, and brother Brigham and I had worked very hard to gather the sap, which labor fell entirely on Brigham, but I kept it a-boiling. We had eaten the last flour the day father left, and had not had a bite all day except what sugar we had eaten and we were very faint, but as night drew nigh we started for the house and to our joy a little robin came flying along and lit on a tall tree near the house. Brigham ran to the house and got the gun, and if I ever prayed in my life, I did then that he might kill the poor little robin. The gun cracked and down came the robin. We soon had it dressed and boiling in the pot, and when we thought it cooked we then wished for flour enough to thicken the broth. Finally brother Brigham got the flour barrel and told me to set a pan on the floor and he held up the barrel and I thumped it with a stick and the flour came out of the cracks and we got two or three spoonfuls and thickened the broth, and then with thanks to God for his mercy, we ate and seemed to have all we wanted, a full meal for two hungry boys on one little robin and two spoonfuls of flour.

We had a good night's rest, and the next morning went to work and worked all day until almost night on the strength of our little robin, when our father came with flour and we were once more happy. Now in my advanced life I can look back upon the days of my boyhood and see the many hardships I had to pass through, and to remember the hardships my father with his family passed through, and who from obscurity have become some of Zion's noblest sons and daughters.[33]

Lloyd Webb of Sugar Hill stated that his ancestors made maple syrup with Phinehas Young. One tree on Sugar Hill tapped by Webb was claimed to have been tapped by Brigham Young over 125 years earlier.[34]

---

Both by tradition and fact the John Young family was, and it remained, very poor, their survival requiring long years of hard labor and denial. Brigham reminisced that he "used to work in the woods logging and driving a team, summer and winter, not half clad, with insufficient food until my stomach would ache.[35] And in a similar vein: "In my youthful days, instead of going to school, I had to chop logs, to sow and plant, to plow in the midst of roots barefooted, and if I had on a pair of pants that would cover me I did pretty well."[36]

John and his sons, in addition to moving into and clearing new land and procuring food for themselves, also hired out to clear and otherwise work the land of others for what little income such employment would bring. One historical account states that as farmers they were not successful. The father bottomed chairs and exhorted, while the sons did odd jobs for the neighboring farmers, but chiefly employed themselves in hunting and fishing. During the harvest season they usually went over the lake to assist the farmers in Romulus.[37] Brigham, commenting on such hire, said that he grew up in an area

> where it often was almost impossible to hire to do a day's work—where a man would have to run and, perhaps, beg to do a day's work; and when the labor was performed, it was frequently worth twice the amount to get the pay, which would generally be only three or four bits.[38]

That Brigham referred several times negatively to the hard, and apparently painful, work of clearing wilderness land indicates that the experience was a trial to him as a young boy. Anyone who has also experienced such labor can understand; working in the forest with hand tools is heavy, man's labor that is both physically punishing and emotionally draining, given the slow, seemingly never-ending nature of such work. Add to that the general poverty, the frequent hunger, and the strict discipline applied by their father, one does not wonder that John Young's sons did not often reflect back on their youth with much joy. Brigham once indicated that he had had bouts with depression, depression apparently common on the frontier in those times.

> I was troubled with that which I hear others complain of, that is, with, at times, feeling cast down, gloomy, and desponding; with everything wearing to me, at times, a dreary aspect . . . I felt lonesome and bad.[39]

Of his older brother Joseph, Brigham said, "For many years no person saw a smile on his countenance."[40]

Brigham, although he was obedient to his parents, hated one aspect of his childhood that he vowed his own children would never have to experience.

> When I was young, I was kept within very strict bounds, and was not allowed to walk more than half-an-hour on Sunday for exercise. The proper and necessary gambols of youth having been denied me, makes me want active exercise and amusement now. I had not a chance to dance when I was young, and never heard the enchanting tones of the violin, until I was eleven years of age; and then I thought I was on the high way to hell, if I suffered myself to linger and listen to it. I shall not subject my little children to such a course of unnatural training, but they shall go to the dance, study music, read novels, and do anything else that will tend to expand their frames, add fire to their spirit, improve their minds, and make them feel free and untrammeled in body and mind.[41]

Here, then, was an experience of his early New York years that abundant evidence indicates had a lasting effect on him—and through him his church—regarding the achievement of a healthy mixture of entertainment and recreation with hard work and the burdens of responsibility.

Still, poverty was the burden that most heavily weighed on Brigham throughout his youth. Brigham recalled that even shoes were considered a luxury. One day, by some fortunate circumstance, he became the possessor of a pair of shoes. His feet, however, were well accustomed to doing without covering, and the shoes were saved for special occasions. When he went to church, Brigham carried them until he was near the place of gathering. They were then donned for the duration of the meeting, "only to be taken off on the return home."[42] Again, he recalled:

> My sisters would make me what was called a Jo Johnson cap for winter, and in the summer I wore a straw hat which I frequently braided for myself. I learned how to make bread, wash the dishes, milk the cows, and make butter. . . . These are about all the advantages I gained in

my youth. I know how to economize, for my father had to do it.[43]

Brigham Young best summed up his family's lot, and how it affected his life and philosophy, many years later.

I have been a poor boy and a poor man, and my parents were poor. I was poor during childhood, and grew up to manhood poor and destitute; and I am acquainted with the various styles of living, and with the different customs, habits, and practices of people; and I do know, by my own experience, that there is no necessity for people being so very poor, if they have judgment, and will rightly use it.[44]

## CHAPTER TWO

# Aspiring to Manhood
# 1817-1824

*"I stopped running, jumping, wrestling and
laying out my strength for naught."*
Brigham Young
Sermon of November 6, 1864
*Journal of Discourses, 10: 360*

In 1817 Brigham Young, then sixteen years old, left home and went on his own. His father had said, "You now have your time; go and provide for yourself."[1] Records indicate that Brigham, having "made up his mind to quit the country and see what he could find to do in the village,"[2] went directly to the vicinity of Auburn, where he may have boarded at first with Susannah and James Little in Aurelius.

Whatever his initial residence, it appears that he "farmed" or "bound" himself out to various families in and around Auburn for his board and a small stipend.[3] He was hired as a "chore boy" on the Reed and Wadsworth farms on West Genesee Street in Auburn,[4] and worked in what was claimed to be the "oldest asparagus bed in the county on a corner of that town's Grover Street.[5]

Brigham was soon joined by Lorenzo and Joseph—and possibly by Phinehas. Lorenzo, then only ten years old, arrived during the winter of 1817-18 and apprenticed himself to James Little, and Joseph arrived in the spring of 1818 and "let [himself] to Mr. James Little for service, and worked two years for him for Six Dollars per month, or $72.00 per year."

Records indicate that Phinehas married Clarissa Hamilton in Auburn in 1818 and that he lived in Mentz (or Haydenville), a village between Aurelius and Port Byron where Brigham was to reside a few years later.[6]

---

Auburn in 1817 was a bustling frontier town situated on the well-traveled Seneca Turnpike. It was a plain, rather Dutch-looking village and its muddy streets were choked with a never-ending wave of immigrants. Land speculation ran high and the village fathers, prodded by local land barons, opened new streets to meet the fresh demand for building lots. It was a boom town with new buildings going up virtually overnight.

Auburn held great promise for the future. Its thousand or so residents worked clearing land, or found employment in the mills or in the various shops, stores, and taverns along Genesee Street. This was the town's principal avenue, the most traveled in spite of its mud and lack of sidewalks. At least thirty shops and six taverns displayed their colorful sign-boards.[7]

One of these buildings, near what is now Osborne Street, housed the woodworking shop of John C. Jeffries, who advertised "Chair Making, Sign Painting and Gilding," and who, in a local newspaper dated November 6, 1816, ran this ad:

## HOUSE AND SIGN PAINTING

John C. Jeffries,
Respectfully informs the Citizens of the village of Auburn, that he will carry on the business of CARRIAGE, SIGN AND HOUSE PAINTING in a neat and workmanlike manner - and has engaged a competent hand from Albany, where he has been employed in the first houses in that city. All orders therefore in the above lines, will be thankfully received, and punctually attended to.
Auburn, Nov. 6, 1816                                                8tf

N. B. All kinds of Chairs, well finished and neatly painted, on hand for sale as usual.

*The Advocate of the People*
Auburn, May 28, 1817

It was apparently to this Mr. Jeffries that Brigham Young, at the age of sixteen, was apprenticed to learn the trades of carpenter, painter, and glazier.[8] Of his early apprenticeship, Brigham later recalled:

> The first job my boss gave me was to make a bedstead out of an old log that had been on the beach of the Lake for years, water-logged and watersoaked. Said he—"There are tools, you cut that log into right lengths for a bedstead. Hew out the side rails, the end rails and the posts; get a board for a head board, and go to work and make a bedstead." And I went to work and cut up the log, split it up to the best of my ability, and made a bedstead that, I suppose, they used for many years. I would go to work and learn to make a washboard, and make a bench to put the wash tub on, and to make a chair.[9]

One of Brigham's early assignments as Jeffries's assistant was to do painting in the home of Judge Elijah Miller. On July 25, 1816, Miller had purchased from William Bostwick four acres of land on the "triangle" south of the Western Exchange Hotel between South and William streets in Auburn. In the course of a year, Miller had a fine two-story brick house erected on the site. In the fall of 1817 Jeffries was employed to "paint the woodwork, [and he] brought with him the renowned Brigham Young, then a journeyman of his, to assist him."[10] The Miller (now Seward) House on South Street, today one of the finest museums of its type in upstate New York, boasts an ornate mantelpiece reputed to be the work of Brigham Young.[11]

Owners of several old houses in Auburn today claim the distinction of having a "Brigham Young mantelpiece." During the period in which these houses were built, fireplaces were installed in several rooms in each house for heat, and the best rooms of a house had decorative mantels to enhance the beauty of their architecture. There is speculation that during the winter months craftsmen such as Brigham Young produced a supply of these beautifully handcrafted mantel-pieces in the shop, and in turn sold them to other local carpenters and builders. Many of the mantels bore striking similarities in workmanship.

Brigham also worked on construction of the Auburn Theological Seminary and the home of one of its trustees. (The cornerstone of this Presbyterian institution was laid "with great formality" on the afternoon of May 11, 1820, and subsequently opened that October with eleven students.) Young nearly lost his life one day while painting on the roof of the three- to four-story structure. The support he was on gave way and he slid down the roof's incline. Luckily he was able to grab hold of the wooden eaves trough as he went over the roof's edge, where he dangled until rescuers brought ladders and helped him down.[12]

One of the seminary's first trustees was "Squire" William Brown, who lived in a house at the corner of South and Grover streets, opposite the Miller (Seward) House. Brigham is reputed to have worked on the construction of Brown's house as a carpenter, painter, and glazier.

About 1854 the Brown House was purchased by Charles Hutchinson. It later became the residence of his daughter, Alice J., and David M. Dunning, whom she married in 1871. Dunning's mother, Jane, was the daughter of Joseph Wadsworth, and Dunning was born in the old Wadsworth home (Joseph Wadsworth House) on West Genesee Street where Brigham is reported to have lived and worked for a time.[13]

David, who resided in the Brown House until his death on August 24, 1940, spoke proudly of Brigham Young's connection with his family.

> My grandfather [Joseph Wadsworth] always spoke very highly of Brigham as an energetic, active and capable young man. His living there was generally known in the family and often mentioned during our life there.[14]

The Brown House itself was a fine example of Federal architecture. When David Dunning died in 1940, the property was sold to J. Reynolds Wait.[15] The house was then rented to a succession of tenants, fell into decay, and was finally demolished in 1974.

The LDS church has received as gifts a number of wooden artifacts said to have been made by Brigham Young. For example, Mr. Wait made a gift of several mantelpieces, through his friend Karl Butler, to the LDS church as specimens of Young's handiwork. One representative mantelpiece is presently a fixture in the high council room of the Latter-day Saint chapel in Ithaca, New York.

Dunning told of a water-powered woodworking shop on the nearby bank of Crane Brook where Brigham apparently made furniture. Dunning's widow owned a cherry desk said to have been made in this little shop. Also given to the LDS church, the desk is plain and sturdy, rather chaste in design, but nonetheless of fine workmanship.

In still another account, Sylvester Matthews reported that after the Brown House was completed, Brigham applied for work at the old cabinet shop across Grover Street, on the present site of Memorial City Hall. Brigham was told by the proprietor, Colonel John Richardson, that he already had two apprentices. One Richardson descendant said, however, that Brigham did indeed eventually secure work with Colonel Richardson in his "furniture factory."[16]

Brigham told of having assisted in building the first meat market in Auburn. The market, located on the west side of the North Street bridge over the Owasco Outlet, was opened by Edward Patten (of Onondaga Hill) in 1820.[17]

Brigham Young summed up this early "career," and hinted at the maturity he had gained in the process, in a sermon decades later.

> Among various other occupations I have been a carpenter, painter and glazier, and when I learned my trades and worked, both as journeyman and master, if I took a job of painting and glazing, say to the amount of one pound sterling, or five dollars, and through my own carelessness in any manner injured the work or material, I considered it my duty to repair the injury at my own expense.[18]

There is no doubt that Brigham took pride in his carpentry. He once wrote an acquaintance from the New York days:

> I felt amused and interested in your statement that a chair made by me would occupy a place in your Centennial supper to be held next Tuesday. I have no doubt that many other pieces of furniture and other specimens of my handiwork can be found scattered about your section of the country, for I have believed all my life that, that which was worth doing was worth doing well, and have considered it as much a part of my religion to do honest, reliable work, such as would endure, for those who employed me, as to attend to the services of God's worship on the Sabbath.[19]

It was therefore in Auburn, first as a mere "chore boy" and then as a "carpenter, painter, and glazier," that Brigham became a man and began to establish for himself the principles and disciplines that were to guide him with excellent effect for the rest of his life. Of that "arriving" he reminisced that

> a year had not passed away before I stopped running, jumping, wrestling and laying out of my strength for naught; but when I was seventeen years of age, I laid my strength in planing a board, or in cultivating the ground to raise something from it to benefit myself. I applied myself to those studies and pursuits of life that would commend me to every good person who should become acquainted with me, although, like other young men, I was full of weakness, sin, darkness and ignorance. . . . I sought to use language on all occasions, that would be commendable, and to carry myself in society, in a way to gain for myself the respect of the moral and good among my neighbors.[20]

## CHAPTER THREE

# Work, Marriage, Lean Times
# 1824-1832

*"He was poor but had enough to be comfortable. He . . . was a hard working man. . . . he was very handy with tools and had a trade; he was a carpenter and joiner. . . . there could scarcely be a more kind and affectionate husband than he was."*

Canandaigua Republican Times
September 7, 1857

**B**righam Young was not to establish his career in Auburn as a master carpenter, apparently because he was unable to find enough work to sustain himself. His search for work led him to the nearby town of Port Byron, on the Erie Canal seven miles north of Aurelius, "where he got in with an old chair repairer and general tinkerer who gave him a job with a $7 a month tenant house and an antique vehicle to collect furniture for repairs."[1] Another account states that he "worked about any odd jobs he could get. At Port Byron, in this county, he painted boats."[2] Apparently starting as a painter, he became involved in other aspects of boat building, and eventually was given the charge of other men.[3] Many years later, it was related that the proprietors of the boatyard said Brigham "would do more work in a given time and secure more and better work from his help without trouble than any man they have ever employed."[4]

One "odd job" performed by Brigham in Port Byron may have won him a life-long friend and admirer. Longtime Port Byron merchant David B. Smith, for whom Brigham had painted a "Goods for Sale" sign, noted that he "was as fine a specimen of young manhood" as he had ever known and he was "one that would have made his mark in whatever community his lot might have been cast."[5]

On May 26, 1823, Brigham purchased a one-acre lot in Port Byron from Aholiab Buck for sixty dollars. The deed located the lot "on the west side of the Owasco Creek lying between the Montezuma Turnpike and the Erie Canal."[6] There is no other mention of the property, but future events indicate that Brigham never made use of it.

Brigham also gained employment in a pail factory operated by Charles Parks at Haydenville, or Mentz, a short distance south of Port Byron.[7] According to William Hayden,

> The factory on the outlet of Owasco lake, which in late years was known as Hayden's woolen mill, was at the time of my acquaintance with Brigham Young begun, a manufactory of wooden pails. . . . He found employment in the pail factory at 50 cents a day, with the understanding that he "should do such work as might be required of him."[8]

Brigham may have made his first attempt at inventing while at the pail factory. Hayden reported that he built a water-powered contraption for grinding paint.[9] Hayden further recounted that Brigham's quick action and willingness to take charge once saved the factory from destruction by fire.[10] Brigham's ingenuity and industry apparently won him the praise of his employer. Again, according to Hayden, Brigham "was first employed at painting pails, the work being done in a manner so satisfactory as to call forth many compliments from the proprietor, Mr. Parks to dispense with the services of one man while the work itself would be better done."[11]

Information about Brigham Young's romance with Miriam Works is somewhat confused owing to the sketchy and conflicting sources that exist. Whatever the exact details, the following account is pieced together from all the known evidence.

Miriam Angeline Works was the second child of Asa and Jerusha Works, and was born in Aurelius on June 7, 1806. Asa Works, like Brigham's father a Revolutionary War veteran, had come to this area from Worcester, Massachusetts. According to Susa Young Gates, Miriam was "a beautiful blonde with blue eyes and wavy hair; gentle and loveable."[12]

Brigham and Miriam may have met at a dance in Aurelius, or were perhaps introduced through mutual acquaintances in Haydenville. That they met at a dance is plausible, considering that they both lived near Half Acre, an Aurelius crossroads on the Seneca Turnpike that boasted three taverns where respectable community dancing parties were periodically held. According to local folklore, Brigham attended such social gatherings.[13] Again, whatever may have been the case, Miriam returned Brigham's attentions and they were married on October 5, 1824. The *Cayuga Patriot* belatedly printed a brief notice of the marriage on November 3, 1824, interestingly followed by notice of the marriage of Brigham's youngest sister, Louisa.

> Married.
> On the 5th ult.[October] by Gilbert Weed, Esq. Mr. Brigham Young, to Miss Marian [*sic*] Works, daughter of Mr. Asa Works.

On the morning of Sixth ult, [October] by Gilbert Weed, Esq. Mr. Joel Sanfort [*sic*] to Miss Louisa Young.[14]

Details as to where Brigham and Miriam exchanged vows and where they spent their honeymoon are also conflicting. Elizabeth Churchill Webb, granddaughter of Gilbert Weed, who officiated at the wedding, stated that the ceremony took place at the Weed tavern near Auburn.[15] According to another account, Weed performed the ceremony at the tavern of James Pine in Port Byron.[16] Marion

Knapp reported that the couple spent their honeymoon at her home at Haydenville,[17] and Howard Power reported that old-timers recalled that the Youngs stayed in a modest log dwelling at the rear of his farm three-fourths of a mile northeast of Aurelius.[18]

One account covering the entire event, perhaps inaccurate if not fanciful, has survived. According to William Hayden,

> while Brigham was employed at the pail factory, a young woman friend of the proprietor's family who was in the custom of visiting there was introduced to him and this was the beginning of Brigham Young's acquaintance with a very worthy young woman, Angeline Works. As their acquaintance ripened, her visits were thought to be a little more frequent, or, at least, they were noticed more. Her long walk home in the evening would have been monotonous, not to say dangerous, if taken alone, therefore, Brigham, with characteristic gallantry, used to accompany her, her home being distant from his boarding place about four miles, or one mile south of Throopsville.
>
> As might have been expected, only a few of these long walks were enjoyed before arrangements for marriage were entered into and on the morning of the wedding day, while we were at our breakfast, a sharp rap called my father to the door. A short conversation ensued, after which father and his visitor went to the barn and soon we saw Brigham drive out of the yard with our horse and wagon. My mother wished to know why father would allow Brigham to take his horse when his rule was to refuse it to all young men. His reply was that Brigham was not like most young men, for he knew enough to use a horse and not abuse it and, beside that, he was going to bring home a bride.[19]

Perhaps the real story of their marriage will never be known. Interviewed in 1876, Brigham said that while he lived in New York State he had married into a family there, "but it is long ago, so very long ago, that I have forgotten almost all about them."[20] Forgetful, or reticent, as he may have been, evidence indicating that Brigham loved his first wife, and cared for her as best he could as long as she lived, is borne out later in this chapter.

William Hayden reported that as "wedding trips to Washington or other distant places had not at that time been invented . . . in a few days Brigham and his wife were installed in a house opposite the pail factory which is still standing."[21]

> The house where Brigham lived . . . was a frame building sixteen feet wide and twenty-four feet in length, a short story and a half high, devoid of paint inside or out, standing with the end toward the road nearly opposite the old factory and directly in front of the old bridge crossing the outlet between Throopsville and Port Byron.
>
> In the east end was an old-fashioned fire place and large chimney, with stairway on one side and a small pantry on the other. Two rooms were partitioned off on the west end for bedrooms, being about seven feet square. The intervening space was parlor, sitting room, dining room and kitchen combined. The lower rooms of the house were roughly plastered; but were without the luxury of a cellar.[22]

This is apparently the same home, owned by Marion Knapp, where Brigham and Miriam reportedly also spent their honeymoon. Mrs. Knapp went on to state that the couple lived there during the first months of their marriage while Brigham worked at the factory across the road.[23]

Little else is known regarding Brigham and Miriam's lives together during the five years they made their home in the Aurelius-Port Byron vicinity—other than that their first daughter, Elizabeth, was born on September 26, 1825, reportedly in Port Byron. Somewhat more was recorded regarding Brigham Young himself during that period— recollections published decades later after Brigham had become famous.

William Hayden recalled that Brigham

> was a great favorite with the small boys then quite numerous in the pail factory neighborhood. Having on this occasion collected a pack of kids of which I was one, he took them onto the bridge and arranged them in a row

and after making them a short speech on good manners, for boys, he ordered all to take their hats in their hands and do as he did, and to bello as loudly as possible. "Now, all at once, swing your hats and hurrah for Andrew Jackson."[24]

Brigham was also a great reader. The Bible received the first and greatest share of his attention, after which ancient history and the weekly newspaper claimed his interest, dailies not being printed at that time. Sunday afternoons, when the weather was suitable, he would usually be seen with his books occupying a rustic seat under a large sycamore tree beside the creek.[25]

Hayden, with the apparent embellishment typical of his other accounts, described one incident that indicated two traits of Brigham Young in later years: his criticisms of others could be devastating, and he often stated that although "he was not a fighting man," if forced he would oblige—in self defense or in defense of his church.

> Schoolhouse debating societies were in vogue in those days, and one being announced to occur in the schoolhouse nearby, Brigham was invited to attend. He went with the intention of being a listener only, but was drawn in as a participant, and at the close was looked upon as the lion of the evening.
> In the course of his argument, he drew the portrait of a would-be smart young man so perfectly that one in the audience took it all to himself, and springing to his feet he threw off his coat, declaring his intention to whip Brigham there and then. Older ones persuaded the young man to keep quiet, though he repeated his threat to do the whipping as soon as they were out of doors. Brigham merely noticed the threat by saying that he was not a fighting man, but that if attacked he should assuredly defend himself and that the result must determine who had received the whipping. He was not attacked.[26]

In 1828 the Brigham Youngs abruptly pulled stakes and moved to Oswego, New York, on the shore of Lake Ontario, twenty-eight miles north of Port Byron. Very little is known of that brief sojourn. In one letter (written in 1853), Brigham stated that he "built a large tannery" there;[27] and in letters exchanged in 1860 between Brigham and Hiram McKee (a Methodist minister), it is evident that the two had together attended religious meetings and had talked religion while both lived in Oswego. Of more the record is silent.[28]

As best as can be determined, the Youngs remained in Oswego for less than a year, then in the spring of 1829 moved to Mendon, New York, near Palmyra, some fifty-seven miles to the southwest. Again, as with the sudden moved to Oswego, the record is silent as to why. It can only be surmised that Brigham's father (and other members of the family) having recently moved to Mendon, Brigham's expectation of economic improvement, or his continuing search for the right church had something to do with this decision.

---

Members of the John Young family began to converge on the vicinity of Mendon as early as 1825. The first was Susannah Little. Widowed in 1822 when husband James was killed in a wagon accident, Susannah remained in Aurelius until about 1825, when she moved to Canandaigua, New York, a beautiful town at the end of Canandaigua Lake, nine miles southeast of Mendon.[29] She later married William B. Stilson, and the Stilsons, with four children, remained in the Canandaigua-Mendon vicinity until at least 1832.[30]

Rhoda, with her husband John P. Greene, a Methodist minister, moved from Watertown, Jefferson County, New York, to the Mendon vicinity (Bloomfield, seven miles southwest) as early as 1826, if brother Phinehas's account of visiting them there that year is accurate. Whatever the exact date, the Greenes were in Mendon by the time the 1830 U. S. census was taken.[31]

Father John Young moved from Tyrone to Mendon in 1827. There he purchased eight acres of land just south of town.[32]

Phinehas, by then a Methodist minister, moved with his wife, Clarissa, and their five children to Cheshire, Ontario County, south of Canandaigua, for three years, then moved to the Mendon area in the spring of 1829.[33] Louisa, of whom little else is known, was, with her husband, Joel Sanford, and their five children, a resident of Mendon when the 1830 census was taken.[34]

Lorenzo may have lived in Mendon briefly. Following the death of James Little, with whose family he had resided for several years, Lorenzo left Aurelius, visited his brothers Phinehas and John, Jr. at Hector (east of Tyrone, fourteen miles by land around the tip of Seneca Lake), for a short period, then returned to Aurelius, where he apprenticed as a blacksmith. His hopes to be a blacksmith were dashed when he was seriously injured lifting a log, and he once again left Aurelius to take up residence in Watertown where sister Rhoda Greene and family lived.[35] He married Persis Goodall in Watertown (on June 26, 1826), apparently remained in Watertown for an undetermined period, then moved with his family to Mendon for a brief time—if Phinehas remembered correctly. He then returned to Hector in November 1828.[36]

Little is known of the whereabouts of others of the John Young family during the period in discussion. Nancy Kent lived with her husband and children in Tyrone until at least 1832. Fanny also lived in Tyrone. Apparently she divorced her first husband, Robert Carr, and later married Roswell Murray. The couple may have moved to the Mendon vicinity by 1832, judging by church records.[37] John Jr., a Methodist preacher, labored in the vicinity of Hector, and Joseph, also a preacher, labored in Kingston, Ontario, Canada, until his conversion to Mormonism in 1831; he then moved to Mendon for a brief time.[38]

---

After their arrival in Mendon it is believed that Brigham and his family briefly lived with John, Sr., then moved into a building, built by Brigham, on the southwest corner of the cheese factory and Mendon-Ionia roads."[39] Evidence, and tradition, indicate that the structure served as home, mill, and place of business. Historian Anah B. Yates stated that Brigham

> following his trade at Mendon . . . built the fine old house still standing and occupied on the Hutchinson farm; he and his family occupying a log house farther up the road. He put up a saw mill on the little creek (where now water cress and forget-me-nots grow in profusion and brook trout are very plentiful in the Spring), and when business was dull made up the lumber, felled by his brothers, into chairs and baskets, that they sold from house to house throughout the country during the winter months.[40]

According to John D. Lynn, an old-time Mendon resident, Brigham operated a basket-making shop in the rear of his house. He went on to state:

> At the eastern end of this farm a large spring pours out of the foot of the hill, forming the source of a beautiful trout stream now frequented by discriminating sportsmen of Rochester. Brigham conveyed this water, through a duct of hollow logs, to an overshot wheel of his own construction, to which he fastened one end of a crosscut saw and, seated on a stump, he held the other end of the saw and watched the waterpower do the work of preparing his lumber for the shop.[41]

J. Sheldon Fisher, local historian and archeologist, has substantiated that Brigham operated a mill on the same stream described by Yates and Lynn. His research reveals that Brigham built a sizeable undershot water wheel, fed by water from the stream, now known as Trout Creek, which powered a lathe with which he turned wood for chairs, other furniture, and spinning wheels. (Fisher established a museum at nearby Fishers, New York, which contains the lathe Brigham used, bits and pieces of furniture, broken crockery and dishes, and even bricks engraved with the letter "B".)

George Washington Allen recorded that as a boy he was once sent "on an errand to Brigham's house."

> His house and shop stood some 80 rods from the highway, nothing but a footpath led to it. . . . I followed this path which lay along the side of a beautiful little stream of clear water noted for the speckled trout it contained. A dam had been thrown across this stream and a sufficient water power obtained to run a turning lathe in his shop.
>
> On arriving at the house and shop I ascended a rickety outside stair case and was bidden to come in. Pulling a leather string and lifting a wooden latch, enabled me to open the door and I entered.
>
> There was only one room in the house, which served for a bedroom-kitchen-sitting room and parlor. . . . There was a bed in one corner, a cupboard for dishes in another, a table and a few splint bottom chairs.[46]

Miriam gave birth to a second daughter, Vilate, on June 1, 1830.[43] Later that year Brigham and his family moved to "Number Nine," a rural community a few miles west of Canandaigua, and into a small house owned by Jonathan Mack, a respected farmer in the community.[44] The house was situated on the west side of what is now Woolhouse Road, opposite the residence of Mr. Mack. Brigham said, "I helped to finish his new house, so that he moved into it before I left the place."[45]

The reason for the move to "Number Nine" is not known. Perhaps it was for the purpose of building the new Mack home. He also worked for wages in the fields of other farmers. Heber C. Kimball recalled that

> Brother Brigham and myself used to work hard, side by side, for fifty cents a day and board ourselves; we had seventy-five cents a day when we worked in the hayfield; we would work from sunrise to sunset, and until nine o'clock at night if there was sign of rain. We would rake and bind after a cradler for a bushel of wheat a day, and chop wood, with snow to our waist for eighteen cents a cord, and take our pay in corn at seventy-five cents a bushel.[46]

The family returned to Mendon in 1832.

Poverty stalked Brigham and his family. He left the Port Byron area owing several debts, and he continued to incur debts in Mendon and Canandaigua. A story is told of how Brigham once approached farmer George Hickox (of Canandaigua) about borrowing a dollar. "Chop wood with me and earn it," was Hickox's reply. On another occasion Brigham owed Hickox a bill and made a dozen chairs to satisfy the account.[47] According to a document found in the University of Rochester archives, he paid off another debt with twenty chairs and some carpentry work.

> $18.50 On the first day of April for value received I promise to pay Milton Sheldon or bearer Eighteen dollars & Fifty cents with Interest - Ten dollars of it to be paid in good Kitchen Chairs at Fifty cents a piece, well done off painted & bottomed according to the usual mode of doing off such chairs-------
> Mendon          March 16th 1830
>                                   Brigham Young

The note is endorsed:

> June 25th    1830 Received on the within Fourteen dollars
>                  & twenty five cents in making picket fence-----
> June 25th    Received on the within Two dollars & fifty
>                  cents in framing on A. Parks Barn.[48]

That he ultimately repaid every debt, promptly as in the case of George Hickox, or many years later, is dramatically born out by the record. Before he left Port Byron,

> Mr. Young called upon each of all of his creditors, obtaining from each the amount of his indebtedness and assured each that he would receive the same, he bade them a friendly good-by. Friends in Port Byron occasionally received letters of remembrance from him and in the spring of 1866 a son was sent with a list of such debts, all of which were duly paid with a goodly amount of interest.[49]

The 1866 visit was made by Brigham's son John Willard, who carried a letter detailing debts to be paid both in Port Byron and Mendon.

Salt Lake City
February 7, 1866
Elder John W. Young

My dear son,

The following are a few items of business I wish you to attend to.

A man by the name of Richard Steel kept a drug store about forty years ago in Auburn, N. Y. He had my note for three dollars ($3.00), which I wished to take up; but he couldn't find it, and said that I must be mistaken about it. I offered to pay the amount, but he refused to receive it. Years afterwards, I heard, and do not now recollect how I heard, that he had found that note, I wish it settled. He may be dead, but heir or heirs may be living.

A note of mine, which was drawn August 28th, 1829, at Bucksville, Cayuga Co., seven miles north of Auburn, for thirty-one dollars and fourteen cents, ($31.14), in favor of Aholiab Buck, or bearer, has been presented by Messrs. Holladay and Halsey to me for settlement. My impression is that the note was paid, but was not taken up. If this were so, I would like to find it out. I wish you to ascertain whether Mr. Buck is living, and by whom this note was forwarded here, and to ascertain whether it will be right for me to pay it here, and if I do, whether it will ever get to Mr. Buck, or if he is dead, to his heir or heirs.

The enclosed copy of a letter, which I lately received from Mr. Ezra Sheldon of Mendon, N.Y., explains itself. The note to which reference is made is dated November 26th, 1829, and was drawn in his favor for ten dollars ($10). I find three dollars ($3) endorsed on the back as having been paid June 15, 1851. I wish you to see Mr. Sheldon and pay this note and interest which amount to $32.28.

Give my kind regards to all the folks in that country who may know me.

Your father, Brigham Young
P. S. If you pay any of these notes, pay nothing but simple interest on them at the rate of 7 per cent. B. Y.[50]

John Willard Young arrived in Auburn the morning of March 19, 1866 to settle up. The *Auburn Advertiser Union* of that date noted:

A son of Brigham Young (we didn't learn his number) was in town this morning, and called at a business house in Genesee St. to settle an account by his numerous progenitor some thirty years ago. Brigham is honest in some things, but rather slow. The debt discharged by him was, we understand, for borrowed money.[51]

Aholiab Buck was not there; he had moved to Illinois in 1832.[52] The debt was paid later to his heirs.

At Lima, New York (seven miles southwest of Mendon), John Willard found Ezra Sheldon, who accepted his money, but "acted as if he did not care how soon we left after he got it; but I excused it in a 'childish old man.' "[53]

Brigham sent still another emissary to New York to repay old debts. Preston Nibley, in his *Brigham Young, the Man and His Work*, states that Brigham summoned William W. Riter, who was about to leave for a proselyting mission in England, to his office, pulled a memorandum containing a record of small debts from his desk, and said;

> William, when I left Mendon thirty years ago, I owed these small sums to various people there. I could not pay them. I now wish that you would stop off on your way east and look these people up and pay them the amounts I owe them, if they are still living. If not, find out who their nearest relatives are and pay the money to them.[54]

The debts listed on the memorandum were not enumerated, but they were reportedly for small sums. Perhaps one of the debts was that reported by John D. Lynn, who stated that he once saw a note made by Brigham Young promising to pay the holder "thirty-nine dollars in bushel baskets at one dollar apiece." Brigham left town without redeeming this note, but many years later a messenger from Salt Lake came in and "took it up."[55]

The *Auburn Daily Bulletin*, in 1877, reported still another debt repaid (with interest) by Brigham Young, a board bill of seventeen dollars owed Port Byron tavern proprietor James Pine, "which he paid, thirty-five years later, with two drafts on New York [a New York bank], for $50 each."[56] (It was claimed that this bill was for board and room provided Brigham and Miriam on their wedding day in 1824.)

---

Miriam, like Brigham's mother, suffered from chronic tuberculosis and did not have long to live. It is reported that during her last months Brigham was a devoted husband and father. The *Ontario Republican Times* reported that

> there could scarcely be a more kind and affectionate husband and father than he was, and few men in his circumstances would have provided better for their families. Mrs. Young was sick, most of the time unable to do any kind of work, but she was a worthy woman, and an exemplary Christian; she was well deserving his care and attention, and she had it while she lived in Canandaigua.[57]

Susa Young Gates, in her perhaps somewhat embellished *The Story of Brigham Young,* stated that Miriam was virtually an invalid, and that Brigham had to take part-time jobs so that he could fix breakfast and do the household chores before going to work. Upon returning home he would carry Miriam to the fireplace, prepare the evening meal, clean up, and carry her back to bed.[58]

Miriam died on September 8, 1832, at the age of twenty-six. She was buried in the little cemetery on Boughton Hill Road, where many Mendon pioneers rest. Following her death, Brigham, Elizabeth, and Vilate, the girls aged six and two, respectively, went to live with Heber C. Kimball.[59]

To what extent poverty and continuous moves had an effect on Miriam's poor health and early death can only be surmised. Suffice to state that hers, like that of Brigham's mother, was apparently a hard life with few opportunities for rejoicing. One account, by a young visitor to the Young home in Mendon, indicates that her lot may have been at times miserable. George Washington Allen, sent to ask for payment of a debt, recounted that upon entering he found Miriam alone,

> poorly and thinly clad, having an old black shawl thrown around her shoulders, endeavoring to keep warm over a single stick of wood on the fire in the fireplace.
>
> She was evidently in feeble health. The only person about the premises was a little red haired girl five or six

years old, with a basket gathering chips and bits of wood for fuel. . . .

Mrs. Young said her husband had gone to Miller's corners (Ionia) to attend a quarterly meeting and she did not know when to expect him home. I made known my errand to her. She replied, "I do not know how or when Mr. Young can pay Dr. Sheldon, he had been gone two or three days and left us without fuel, the last stick is on the fire—we have no flour or meat nor anything else in the house to eat. As soon as he comes home he will first have to provide fuel and provision for the family. Dr. Sheldon will have to be patient a little while longer."[60]

Although the above account was made years after the fact, and possibly exaggerated if not contrived, it indicates that to some extent Brigham Young had been caught up in a pursuit that would perpetuate the family's poverty off and on for the next twenty years, and consume much of Brigham's energies for the rest of his life.

## CHAPTER FOUR

# The Young Family and Religion

*"My ancestors were some of the most strict religionists that lived upon the earth."*
Brigham Young
Sermon of August 15, 1862
*Journal of Discourses*, 6: 290

There can be little doubt that both John Young, Sr. and Abigail Howe had "strict religionist" backgrounds, and that they raised up their children in the same tradition. That their example and training had a major effect is demonstrated by the fact that, of the five sons, three became ordained Methodist ministers (before their conversion to Mormonism) and a fourth became president of the Church of Jesus Christ of Latter-day Saints. Additionally, one of the five sisters (Rhoda) married a Methodist minister, and of the ten surviving children, all were eventually baptized as members of the LDS church.[1]

Brigham noted that his parents were devout Methodists "and their precepts of morality were sustained by their good examples."[2] He spoke eloquently of the moral upbringing provided by his parents.

> I was brought up so strict, so firm in the faith of the Christian religion by my parents, that if I had said "Devil," I believed I had sworn very wickedly, no matter on what occasion or under what circumstances this might occur. If I used the name of Devil, I should have certainly been chastised, and that severely. Would my father or mother

allow any of the children to say "Darn it"? Were they ever allowed to say "I vow"? No. If we said either of these words, we should have been whipped for it. I don't say that we did not say such things when out of the sight of father and mother; but if by any means it came to their ears, we were sure to be chastised.

Did I ever hear a man swear in my father's house? No, never in my life. I never heard my father or any person about his premises swear as much as to say "Darn it," or "Curse it," or "the Devil.". . . My mother, while she lived, taught her children all the time to honour the name of the Father and the Son, and to reverence the holy Book. She said, "Read it, observe its precepts, and apply them to your lives as far as you can; do everything that is good; do nothing that is evil; and if you see any person in distress, administer to their wants; never suffer anger to arise in your bosoms; for, if you do, you may be overcome by evil." I do not know that I ever wronged my neighbor, even to the value of a pin. I was taught, when a child, not to take a pin from the door-yard of a neighbor, but to carry it into the house and give it to some of the family. Never did my mother or father countenance any of their children in anything to wrong their neighbor or fellow-being, even if they were injured by them. If they have injured me, says my father, let me return good for evil, and leave it in the hand of the Lord; he will bless me for doing right and curse them for doing wrong.[3]

Brigham himself, though not entirely satisfied with the religion of the day, strove to live devoutly. Years later he commented:

From the days of my youth, and I will say from the day I came upon the stage of action for myself, there never was a boy, a man, either old or middle aged, that ever tried to live a life more pure and refined than your humble servant.[4]

Lorenzo corroborated his brother's rather unabashed claim.

Brigham was a [boy] of strictly moral habits as far as I ever knew. I do not think he was ever known to drink or use profane language. He was very industrious and hard working. As to his faults, I never knew of anything particular. I never knew of his having difficulty with his associates or his brothers and sisters. . . . I never knew of his getting angry but once in his youthful days when I thought he was violent.[5]

Brigham recalled: "I was not disposed to attach myself to any church, nor to make a profession of religion, though brought up from my youth amid those flaming, fiery revivals so customary with the Methodists."[6] Nor does it appear that his parents attempted to force his allegiance to any specific sect. He was well acquainted, he said, with all the sects of his day, and made it a practice to attend camp meetings and revivals. Indeed, Brigham's younger brother, Lorenzo Dow, was named after a well-known evangelist of the day. Describing having heard Dow preach, Brigham recalled having been disdainful of the evangelist's apparent shallowness.

I recollect when I was young going to hear Lorenzo Dow preach. He was esteemed a very great man by the religious folks. I, although young in years and lacking experience, had thought a great many times that I would like to hear some man who could tell me something, when he opened the Bible, about the Son of God, the will of God, what the ancients did and received, saw and heard and knew pertaining to God and heaven. So I went to hear Lorenzo Dow. He stood up some of the time, and he sat down some of the time; he was in this position and that position, and talked two or three hours, and when he got through I asked myself, "What have you learned from Lorenzo Dow?" Nothing, nothing but morals. He could tell the people they should not work on the Sabbath day; they should not lie, swear, steal, commit adultery, &c., but when he came to teaching the things of God he was as dark as midnight.[7]

From early on Brigham chafed at efforts to convert him fully to the Methodist faith. "I was labored with diligently by the priests to attach myself to some church in my early life,"[8] he says, and recalls that "priests had urged me to pray before I was eight years old. On this subject I had but one prevailing feeling in mind—Lord, preserve me until I am old enough to have sound judgment, and a discreet mind ripened upon a good solid foundation of common sense."[9] Apparently Brigham learned more about morals, about the gospel, and about getting along with his fellow men from his parents than he did by going to camp meetings and listening to lengthy "fire and brimstone" sermons. He said that he saw children and young men "get religion," but he could not do so until he was twenty-two years old, "and then in order to prevent my being any more pestered about it I joined Methodism."[10]

However, he found Methodism rather mediocre in that members did not follow biblical teachings in their practices. Their attitude toward baptism by immersion was a prime example. "You may be baptized by immersion if you absolutely require it," he was told by Methodist ministers, "but we do not believe in it, but we do believe in giving every person his choice." Brigham retorted, "Well, . . . I believe in it. There are some things required in the doctrine of the Close Communion Baptists which I cannot subscribe to as well as to most of the principles that you hold in your catechisms, and in the tenets of your church, but . . . they believe in baptism by immersion, and I want to be baptized by immersion." He reported that the Methodists finally consented to baptize him in this way.[11]

The religious influence of their parents, coupled with serious Bible study, directed the Young brothers away from old companions and worldly amusements. During Brigham's youth, alcoholism was rampant and temperance advocates sought to remedy the situation by persuading people to sign "temperance pledges." Brigham was asked to sign such a pledge, but he felt no obligation in view of his own sense of propriety. "I recollect my father urged me to," he recalled. Brigham's response was, "No sir. If I sign the temperance pledge I feel that I am bound, and I wish to do just right, without being bound to do it; I want my liberty." He later commented that "I have conceived from my youth up that I could have my liberty and independence just as much in doing right as I could in doing wrong."

Brigham apparently had a strong moral constitution and was not "one of the crowd." When he was offered a drink by a companion he would say, "Thank you, I think it is not good for me!" Taunted further, he would answer, "Thank you, I think I know myself better than you know me."[12]

Lorenzo had similar experiences. Recalling his black-smithing days in Aurelius, he said that at the end of the day the workers would often gather around the center table in the sitting room to while away the evening in a game of cards. Lorenzo was invited to participate, but he declined. He was scorned by his peers because of this, but he remembered the counsel of his father that, although playing cards was an innocent pastime, it could lead to other not-so-innocent vices. He made it clear to his employer, Mr. Munroe, that he did not wish to play cards, that he preferred to be left alone to study his scriptures.[13]

Phinehas's discipline was stronger still. He recalled that he became a "born-again" Christian in the fall of 1823. "I forsook all my former associates, and commenced praying and fasting, and watching every weakness of my nature, and the more I prayed the more I saw my weakness and felt my dependence on God."[14]

Almost as if moved simultaneously by the spirit, in a short period at least three of the Young brothers made serious commitments for Christ. Phinehas, converted in 1823, at age twenty-five, was licensed as a Methodist minister in 1824.[15] Brigham, after years of hanging back, "became serious and religiously inclined" in 1823, the same year as Phinehas's conversion. "Soon after this I attached myself to the Metho-dist Church."[17] John, Jr., aged thirty-four, received his license as a Methodist preacher in 1825.[16] Joseph also became a Methodist preacher, and was actively so engaged as early as 1830, but the date of his ordination is not clear.[18]

Only Lorenzo, seventeen in 1824, could not yet make his decision, try as he might. When he arrived in Hector in 1822 following the death of James Little, a Methodist revival (typical of those being held throughout central New York at the time) was in process. Religious fervor was high and as far as he knew every young person in the neighborhood but himself professed to "receive a saving change of heart." At a point in each of the nightly meetings it was the custom to request those who were seeking religion to come forward "to be prayed for." One evening, when the usual invitation was given for the penitent to come forward to the anxious seat, Lorenzo gave way to the spirit of the occasion and went forward with the others. After a lengthy prayer, all but Lorenzo professed to have received a "change of heart."

Following the meeting, Elder Gilmore, the leading minister, proposed that anyone interested should retire to a private home with Lorenzo and continue to pray until he was converted. This was done, and the praying continued until two o'clock in the morning with no evident result. The lad was finally given up as a reprobate. Elder Gilmore told him he had "sinned away the day of grace," asserting that he would never offer another prayer for him. Lorenzo therefore returned to Aurelius to be introduced to his scornful blacksmith peers without having been saved, but devout nonetheless.[19]

The Young brothers experienced a variety of faith-promoting events in Hector. Phinehas recalled a "very singular manifestation".

> I was at a prayer meeting at the house of Israel Pease, in the town of Hector, Tompkins County, New York; the congregation were mostly praying for sanctification; I felt like one alone, for I could pray for nothing but to become holy, and I had got in one corner, as much alone as possible, when all of a sudden I saw a body of light, above the brightness of the sun, descending towards me; in a moment it filled me with joy unutterable: every part of my system was perfectly light and perfectly happy. I soon arose and spake of the things of the kingdom of God, as I had never spake before. I then felt satisfied that the Lord had heard my prayer, and my sins were forgiven.
>
> Soon after this, while at home, I was called to see a young woman in the neighborhood, who had long been sick of consumption. The messenger said the lady was dying, and her friends wished me to come as soon as convenient. I called on my brother John, who lived on the way, and asked him to accompany me, which he very readily did.

We soon arrived at the house. On entering, we found the family and friends weeping, and the young woman, to all appearance, breathing her last. I stepped to the bedside and adjusted the pillows of the dying girl, as she seemed to respire with great difficulty.

At this moment her mother approached me, and asked me if I thought she had a sense of her suffering. I replied, "I cannot say; she appears to be about through with the struggle." She then said, "Will you pray?" I immediately knelt and commenced to invoke my Father in heaven in her behalf, asking him to ease her out of this world of sorrow, and take her to a world of bliss.

After praying thus a few moments I felt a check on my spirit, and a voice whispered to me, "Pray for her recovery." I immediately commenced praying that she might be restored to health, and almost the same minute the same voice said, "Lay hands on the sufferer and rebuke the disease." I did not wait to think of the probable result, but arose without saying Amen, went to the bedside, laid my hands on the dying girl, and bade the power of the destroyer to flee, and said, in the language of the Savior, arise and be made whole. (Here I would say that I had never seen anything of the kind in my life, but had always believed the people were living far beneath their privileges.) The girl arose as one from the dead, and sat up in bed and praised God with a loud voice, and soon became a hearty and healthy woman, and, as far as I know, is still living and well: her name was Mary Webley.

Lorenzo recalled a similar incident involving his sister Fanny:

I once knew my brother John and Calvin Gilmour, a brother Methodist, to leave their work and travel on foot over to the town of Tyrone, a distance of 24 miles, to administer to my sister Fanny, who they had heard lay at the point of death. They all believed in the gift of healing and through faith in the administration, my sister recovered. My father was very earnest and sincere in religion, and when he embraced Mormonism it was with his whole soul.[21]

Following his spiritual experience in Hector, Phinehas was sent to labor in the village of Cheshire, Ontario County (a few miles south of Canandaigua), "which was said to be the wickedest place in western New York. I was very successful in my labors, and soon raised up a branch of forty-five members, and then returned home, after an absence of forty-one days."[22] Phinehas then settled his affairs in Hector and moved his family to Cheshire, where he remained for three years, "laboring for the support of [his] family,"[23] following which,

> having understood that others of my father's family were going there, I concluded to sell out and move to Mendon, which I did in the spring of 1829. About this time my father, brother Lorenzo and others of my father's family, moved into the town. We immediately opened a house for preaching, and commenced teaching the people according to the light we had; a reformation commenced, and we soon had a good society organized, and the Lord blessed our labors. The Baptist Church, with their minister, all seemed to feel a great interest in the work: the reformation spread, and hundreds took an interest in it.[24]

By accident or design, the convergence of the John Young family at Mendon made them all perfectly susceptible to conversion to Mormonism.

View of Whitingham, Vermont, birthplace of Brigham Young.

Cold Brook, near Smyrna, New York, where the John Young, Sr., family resided between 1802 and 1813.   *Longin Lonczyna, Jr.*

Tree said to mark the spot where John Young, Sr., built the family home near Tyrone, New York, in 1815.
*Longin Lonczyna, Jr.*

Course of the Erie Canal at Port Byron, New York, photographed in 1942.   *Photo by John D. Giles, courtesy LDS Church Archives*

Auburn Theological Seminary, Auburn, New York. Brigham Young worked on the construction of this building in 1820.
*Courtesy Kenneth Wright*

Painting of the ruins of the furniture shop owned by Joseph Wadsworth on Crane Brook, on the western outskirts of Auburn, New York. Brigham Young is said to have worked in this shop. *Longin Lonczyna, Jr.*

Print of the Miller (later Seward) House, Auburn, New York, constructed in 1817 for Judge Elijah Miller, William H. Seward's father-in-law. Brigham Young stated that he helped paint this house. *Courtesy Seward House*

Brown (later Hutchinson, then Dunning) House, Auburn, New York. The house stood on South Street across from the Miller (Seward) House on the present site of the New York Telephone Company office.  *Courtesy Cayuga County Historian's Office*

Joseph Wadsworth House (later owned by the parents of David M. Dunning), west of Auburn, New York, near Aurelius, on West Genesee Street Road (old Seneca Turnpike). An example of one of the Federal Style houses Brigham Young may have worked on. House was torn down in 1974.

KNOW ALL MEN BY THESE PRESENTS, THAT WE *Joseph Young, Albrigmen B. Munro and Brigham Young* all of *Aurelius in Cayuga County*

are held and firmly bound unto the People of the State of New-York, in the SUM of *One Thousand Dollars* Current Money of said State, to be paid to the said People: To the which payment well and truly to be made, we do bind ourselves, and each of us, our and each of our Heirs, Executors, and Administrators, jointly and severally, firmly by these Presents. Sealed with our Seals, dated the *Fifth* Day of *December* in the Year of our LORD, one thousand eight hundred and *twenty two* and of our Independence the *Forty Seventh*

THE CONDITION OF THIS OBLIGATION IS SUCH, That if the above bounden *Joseph Young* Administrat*or* of all and singular the Goods, Chattels and Credits of *James Little late of Aurelius in S. County* deceased, do make, or cause to be made, a true and perfect Inventory of all and singular the Goods, Chattels and Credits of the said deceased, which have, or shall come to the hands, possession, or knowledge of the said *Joseph Young* or into the hands or possession of any other person or persons for the said *Joseph Young* and the same so made, do exhibit, or cause to be exhibited, into the office of the Surrogate of the County of *Cayuga* at or before the expiration of six calendar months from the date of the above written Obligation, and the same Goods, Chattels and Credits, and all other Goods, Chattels and Credits of the said deceased, at the time of *his* death, which at any time after shall come to the hands or possession of the said *Joseph Young* or into the hands or possession of any other person or persons for the said *Joseph Young* do well and truly administer according to law: And further, when thereunto lawfully required, do make, or cause to be made, a just and true account of Administration: And if it shall hereafter appear that any last Will or Testament was made by the said deceased, and the Executor or Executors therein named, or any person or persons do exhibit the same, and request to have it allowed and approved, then if the said *Joseph Young* being thereunto required do render and deliver the Letters of Administration granted on the Estate of the said deceased, to the Office from which they were issued, then this Obligation to be void and of none effect, or else to remain in full force and virtue.

SEALED AND DELIVERED IN }
THE PRESENCE OF }

*Benjamin L Grayton*

*Joseph Young*

*Albrigmen B Munro*

*Brigham Young*

Photocopy of affidavit, dated December 5, 1822, obligating Joseph Young as the administrator of his brother-in-law James Little's estate, following Little's accidental death on November 15, 1822. Brigham Young's signature (as a witness) may be the earliest of his signatures still in existence.

those distinguished individuals whom I have before mentioned.

I remain your old friend
HAL.

## INTERESTING TO FARMERS.

### LATHYRUS LATIFOLIUS, OR EVERLASTING SWEET PEA.

*Description, Cultivation, and Produce, of a Plant, of this kind of Pea, which is nine years old ; cultivated by the subscriber.*

The plant was transplanted, when a year old, into a rich soil, and commonly kept free from weeds ; but not manured. The vines, the last summer, measured thirty eight feet in circumference, round the plant, and produced fourteen thousand seven hundred and sixty four peas. After the peas were collected, the vines were in a fine green state of vegetation ; and were cut, and weighed twenty two pounds. They were given to cattle, and eaten as freely as green clover. Often cutting, or close feeding will not injure this plant ; as the vines proceed from the crown of the roots, from two to four inches below the surface. The green leaves receive no injury from the winter frost, and affords fine fresh feed, at all times, when the snow does not prevent it. This plant was long since recommended by the celebrated Dr. Anderson, as promising to afford large crops of hay and pasture.

Small quantities of the seed may be had by application to the subscriber.
JAMES LITTLE.
*Aurelius, Cayuga Co.*

*N. B.* A plant of the above kind, four years old, produced at one cutting, fourteen pounds of green vines.

In Congress the Senate on Tuesday

Advertisement in the *Cayuga Patriot*, January 3, 1821, placed by James Little, Brigham Young's brother-in-law.
*Courtesy Cayuga County Historian's Office*

Desk, owned by the Dunning family for several generations, is said to have been made by Brigham Young.   *Longin Lonczyna, Jr.*

Wait House, west of Auburn, New York, near Aurelius, on
West Genesee Street Road. Brigham Young reportedly worked
on this house.    *Longin Lonczyna, Jr.*

Fine workmanship of
early nineteenth-
century craftsmen is
evident in the
staircase and main
entrance to the Wait
House.
*Longin Lonczyna, Jr.*

Mantlepiece in the Wait House, possibly crafted by Brigham
Young.   *Longin Lonczyna, Jr.*

Ramsey (later Westover) Tavern at Half Acre, Aurelius, New York, on the old Seneca Turnpike. Brigham Young may have met Miriam Works here, although they may rather have met at one of the two other taverns that stood at this crossroads in 1824.

Miller Mansion, Ludlowville, New York, built (circa 1817) for Abijah Miller, uncle of Judge Elijah Miller of Auburn. Folklore associates Brigham Young with its construction.

The old Hayden's Woolen Mills, in Haydenville (Mentz), south of Port Byron, New York, was initially a pail factory where Brigham Young worked in about 1824.

Brigham and Miriam Young are said to have lived in this house (since remodeled) in Port Byron, New York.
*Courtesy LDS Church Archives*

Brigham Young is said to have built a wing to the back of this home near Mendon, New York, for his father.

MIRIAM WORKS YOUNG
WIFE OF
BRIGHAM YOUNG
BORN JUNE 7, 1806
AT AUERELIUS, NEW YORK
DIED SEPTEMBER 8, 1832
AT MENDON, NEW YORK

Miriam Works Young was buried in an unmarked grave in Tomlinson's Corners Cemetary, near Mendon, New York. Present monument was placed here by descendants of Brigham Young.

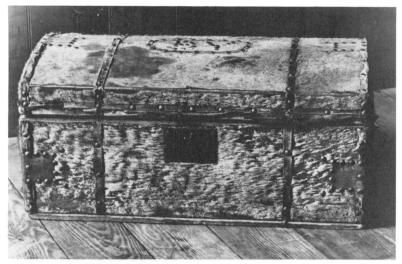

Trunk, with the initials "BY" rivited on the lid, found in the house
Brigham Young lived in near Mendon, New York. On display at
the Valentown Museum, Fishers, New York.
*Longin Lonczyna, Jr.*

Lathe said to have
been made and used
by Brigham Young in
the little sawmill in
back of his father's
home. On display at
the Valentown
Museum, Fishers,
New York.
*Longin Lonczyna, Jr.*

Pastoral scene near Aurelius, New York.
*Photo by John D. Giles, courtesy LDS Church Archives*

Chair said to have
been made by
Brigham Young in
his mill/workshop at
Mendon, New York.

Armchair, said to have been made by Brigham Young, was preserved by the Hickox family of "Number Nine," west of Canandaigua, New York. On display at the Ontario County Historical Society Museum, Canandaigua.
*Courtesy Ontario County Historical Society Museum*

One of several chimney or foundation bricks excavated by J. Sheldon Fisher at the Brigham Young millsite near Mendon, New York. The letter "B," which in part closely resembles the "B" in Brigham Young's signature, may well have been scribed into the bricks by him.

Brigham and Miriam Young's daughters, Vilate and Elizabeth. Both were born in New York, became Mormons in 1832, and accompanied their father to Ohio, Illinois, and ultimately Utah. *Courtesy LDS Church Archives*

The Young brothers. *From left:* Lorenzo, Brigham, Phinehas,
Joseph, and John.    *Courtesy LDS Church Archives*

Home where Brigham Young is said to have brought his new bride, Miriam Works, in 1824. Home is located on the Owasco Outlet, in Haydenville (Mentz), New York, 1½ miles south of Port Byron. *Courtesy LDS Church Archives*

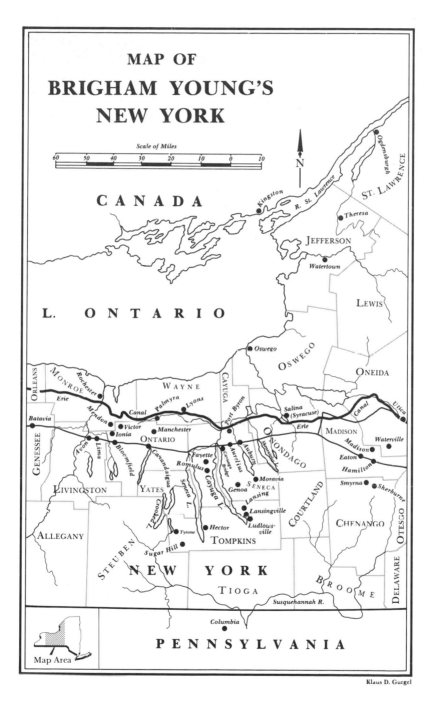

# MAP OF
# BRIGHAM YOUNG'S
# NEW YORK

Scale of Miles

60   50   40   30   20   10   0   10

N

C A N A D A

Ogdensburgh

Kingston

R. St. Lawrence

ST. LAWRENCE

Theresa

L.   O N T A R I O

JEFFERSON

Watertown

LEWIS

Oswego

OSWEGO

ONEIDA

ORLEANS

MONROE

Rochester

WAYNE

CAYUGA

Erie

Palmyra

Lyons

Port Byron

Salina
(Syracuse)

Canal

Utica

Batavia

Mendon

Canal

Erie

MADISON

Madison

Waterville

GENESEE

Victor

Manchester

ONTARIO

Ionia

Avon

Lima

Bloomfield

Canandaigua

Fayette

Aurelius

Auburn

ONONDAGO

Eaton

Hamilton

Romulus

Cayuga Bridge

Cayuga L.

Moravia

SENECA

Smyrna

Sherburne

LIVINGSTON

YATES

Seneca L.

Genoa

Lansing

Lansingville

COURTLAND

CHENANGO

OTSEGO

ALLEGANY

Tyrone

Hector

Ludlows-
ville

TOMPKINS

STEUBEN

Sugar Hill

N E W    Y O R K

TIOGA

B R O O M E

DELAWARE

Susquehannah R.

Columbia

P E N N S Y L V A N I A

Map Area

Klaus D. Gurgel

## CHAPTER FIVE

# Conversion

*"I felt . . . that if I could see the face of a
Prophet . . . I would freely circumscribe
the earth on my hands and knees."*
Brigham Young
Sermon of September 28, 1856
*Journal of Discourses* 4: 104

The coming forth of the Book of Mormon, discovered in September 1827 and first published in March 1830, precipitated the conversion of virtually every member of the John Young family. Just when a member, or members, of the family first heard of the book is somewhat questionable, although Brigham Young and Heber C. Kimball claimed, in separate accounts, that at least eight members of the family (John, Sr., Brigham and Miriam, John P. and Rhoda Greene, Fanny Murray, and Heber and Vilate Kimball) saw a vision on the night of September 22, 1827, the night Joseph Smith, Jr. reported that he received the golden plates of the Book of Mormon at the Hill Cumorah near Palmyra, New York.[1] At the time, Brigham and Miriam were in the vicinity of Port Byron, and the others were in Mendon. Brigham recalled:

> The night the plates were found, there was a great light in the East and it went to the West and it was very bright although there was no moon at the time. I gazed at it in company with my wife. The light was perfectly clear and remained several hours. It formed into men as if

there were great armies in the West; and I then saw in the northwest armies of men come up. They would march to the South West and then go out of sight. It was very remarkable occurrence. It passed on, and continued perhaps about two hours.[2]

Heber Kimball recalled that Vilate, apparently seeing the same manifestation forty-six miles further west, asked her grandfather, "'Father Young, what does all this mean?' He replied in a lively pleased manner, 'Why it's one of the signs of the coming of the son of man.'"[3]

That Brigham had received information, either by vision or otherwise, while still in Port Byron is indicated by the recollection of William Hayden.

> While engaged in boat building, the air became filled with rumors of a new revelation, to the effect that a new Bible written upon golden plates had been dug out of the earth at Palmyra, a canal village twenty-five miles west of Port Byron. Each day brought new accounts of the wonder and each account would differ from its predecessor. Finally Brigham determined to investigate for himself, expecting to be able to expose it as a fraud.
>
> Accordingly, on a Saturday morning he boarded a west-bound canal boat and Sunday morning found him in Palmyra, where he spent the day with those who had been investigating the subject. Becoming interested, he spent several succeeding Sundays in like manner and, instead of exposing the new teaching as a fraud as he had anticipated doing, he became a firm convert to the doctrines there expounded.[4]

The fanciful language and the confusion of the dates, however, makes Hayden's account suspect. Whatever earlier manifestations there might have been, several members of the family had access to a copy (or copies) of the Book of Mormon soon after it was published (on March 26, 1830). At the first conference of the fledgling "Church of Christ," held on June 9, 1830 in Fayette (about thirty-one miles southeast of Mendon), Joseph Smith's brother Samuel was called on a mission to promulgate the Book of Mormon to the people in and around Palmyra. His mission (what can be considered the first actual mission served in the church), brought Samuel to the home of John P. Greene, in Bloomfield—and to Tomlinson's Inn, in nearby Lima, where Phinehas H. Young had stopped for dinner.[5]

Brigham recalled: "I was somewhat acquainted with the coming forth of the Book of Mormon, not only through what I read in the newspapers, but I also heard a great many stories and reports which were circulated as quick as the Book of Mormon was printed, and began to be scattered abroad." He added that he first saw the Book of Mormon that spring, "which brother Samuel H. Smith brought and left with my brother Phinehas H. Young."[6]

Phinehas recorded that one day in April 1830 he was on his way home from preaching in the town of Lima and had stopped at John Tomlinson's inn for dinner when he was approached by Smith. After some conversation, Phinehas agreed to take a copy and read it, "and make myself acquainted with its errors, so that I [could] expose them to the world." After two weeks of intense study, Phinehas, although he still maintained his faith in Methodism, became convinced of the truthfulness of the "Golden Bible."[7]

> On the next Sabbath I was requested to give my views on the subject, which I commenced to do. I had not spoken ten minutes in defence of the book when the Spirit of God came upon me in a marvelous manner, and I spoke at great length on the importance of such a work, quoting from the Bible to support my position, and finally closed by telling the people that I believed the book. The greater part of the people agreed with my views, and some of them said they had never heard me speak so well and with such power.[8]

Phinehas's account, seemingly corroborated by Brigham, that Samuel delivered the Book of Mormon in April 1830 is probably erroneous. Other evidence places the event as following the June 9 church conference in Fayette.[9] Joseph Smith's mother, Lucy Mack Smith, wrote that Samuel started on his mission on June 30, 1830. He traveled as far as Bloomfield, attempting to sell copies of the Book of Mormon, but without much success. However, he succeeded in leaving a copy at the home of John P. Greene, who promised to sell it if he could. Samuel then returned home to Manchester.[10]

Lucy's account goes on to state that Samuel returned to Bloomfield and the Greene home and that Greene said he had been unable to dispose of the copy that Samuel had left earlier. On a third visit Samuel found that although the Greenes had been unable to sell the copy of the Book of Mormon provided, it had served as a means of converting them and others.[11]

Following the meeting at which Phinehas had testified,

> my father . . . took the book home with him, and read it through. I asked him his opinion of it. He said it was the greatest work and the clearest of error of anything he had ever seen, the Bible not excepted.[12]

Brigham, in religion considerably more "circumspect" than he described his father as being, was not so easily convinced. He said to himself:

> "Wait a little while; what is the doctrine of the book, and of the revelations the Lord has given? Let me apply my heart to them"; and after I had done this, I considered it to be my right to know for myself, as much as any man on earth.
>
> I examined the matter studiously for two years before I made up my mind to receive that book. I knew it was true, as well as I knew that I could see with my eyes, or feel by the touch of my fingers, or be sensible of the demonstration of any sense. Had not this been the case, I never would have embraced it to this day; it would have all been without form or comeliness to me. I wished time sufficient to prove all things for myself.[13]

His decision on the Book of Mormon may well have needed the encouragement of a group of Mormon missionaries who came through Mendon in the fall of 1831— about a year after Samuel Smith left copies with John P. Greene and Phinehas Young. According to Brigham they "came to Mendon to preach the Everlasting Gospel, as revealed to Joseph Smith, the Prophet, which I heard and believed."[14]

According to the perhaps somewhat imaginary account of Eunice E. Curtis, after the meeting Brigham hurried home to his wife, who was sick in bed. He went to his room and prayed, "If this religion is true, send the missionaries to my home, that they might pray for my sick wife and also explain the gospel to her." The next evening, as the elders were passing Brigham's home, they were impressed with the tidiness of his yards. Reasoning that any man who had that much pride in his home must be worth visiting, they went in. Brigham had been watching from the window to see if his prayer would be answered. He opened the door and welcomed them in. They administered to his wife and she seemed more at ease. Brigham then told them that he had prayed for them to come, and that he had faith that Miriam could be healed through administration.[15]

Quite by chance, in August 1831, just prior to the visit of the missionaries, Joseph Young returned from Canada for the purpose of recruiting Phinehas to come back to Canada with him so that they might preach their Methodist faith together. Phinehas acquiesced and the brothers proceeded toward Kingston, stopping at nearby Lyons, New York, to visit "an old acquaintance," Solomon Chamberlain, who, apparently unbeknownst to the brothers, had become a Mormon.

> We had no sooner got seated than he began to preach Mormonism to us. He told us there was a church organized, and ten or more were baptized, and every body must believe the Book of Mormon or be lost.[16]

Phinehas had already been introduced to the Church, but Joseph had not. Phinehas went on:

> I told him to hold on, when he had talked about two hours setting forth the wonders of Mormonism—that it was not good to give a colt a bushel of oats at a time. I knew that my brother had but little idea of what he was talking, and I wanted he should have time to reflect; but it made little difference to him, he still talked of Mormonism.
> We tarried a short time with him and then went on our way, pondering upon the things we had heard. This was the first I had heard of the necessity of another

church, or of the importance of re-baptism; but after hearing the old gentleman's arguments on the importance of the power of the holy Priesthood, and the necessity of its restoration in order that the power of the Gospel might be made manifest, I began to inquire seriously into the matter, and soon became convinced that such an order of things was necessary for the salvation of the world.[17]

The brothers went on to Kingston and began their labors, but Phinehas was in too much turmoil. "I . . . told [Joseph] I could not preach, and that I should return home." Before he left Kingston, however, he accepted an appointment to preach at a meeting of Christian Indians. There, after hearing accounts of Indian traditions that seemed to "corroborate the truth of the Book of Mormon," Phinehas was moved to bear "a powerful testimony of the work."[18]

His turmoil continued upon his return home.

I still continued to preach, trying to tie Mormonism to Methodism, for more than a year, when I found that they had no connection and could not be united, and that I must leave the one and cleave to the other.[19]

Regarding events of the fall of 1831, accounts by Brigham, Phinehas, and Heber C. Kimball (all given many years later) either are in conflict or are missing important facts. For example, Phinehas, regarding events upon his return, remembered that

about this time my brother Brigham came to see me, and very soon told me that he was convinced that there was something in Mormonism. I told him I had long been satisfied of that.[20]

The account makes no mention of Mormon missionaries, nor what might have prompted Brigham's interest in the new church. Brigham recalled that "Elders Alpheus Gifford, Elial Strong and others came to Mendon," but he did not elaborate as to exactly where they met, or further identify the other missionaries in the visiting group. Both brothers were vague regarding future events also. However, if Heber's account (published in the *Deseret News* in 1858) is accurate as to details, the puzzle left by Brigham and Phinehas might well be solved, particularly regarding the momentous events soon to come. Heber recounted:

> About three weeks after I joined the Baptist church [Fall 1831], five Elders of the Church of Jesus Christ came from Pennsylvania to the house of Phinehas H. Young, in Victor. Their names were Eleazer Miller, Elial Strong, Alpheus Gifford, Enos Curtis and Daniel Bowen."[21]

The significance of these additional details is soon readily apparent. Brigham's account continues:

> In January, 1832, my brother Phinehas and I accompanied Heber C. Kimball, who took his horses and sleigh and went to Columbia, Pennsylvania, where there was a Branch of the Church. We travelled through snow and ice, crossing rivers until we were almost discouraged; still our faith was to learn more of the principles of Mormonism.
> We arrived at the place where there was a small Branch of the Church; we conversed with them, attended their meetings and heard them preach, and after staying about one week we returned home, being still more convinced of the truth of the work, and anxious to learn of its principles and to learn more of Joseph Smith's mission.[22]

Again, although Brigham gives no hint of why such a trip was made, Heber's account clearly indicates that he, Phinehas, and Heber traveled to Columbia to receive further instructions and inspiration from one or more of the missionaries who had visited them the previous fall.

Brigham went on to report that

> immediately after my return home from Pennsylvania I took my horse and sleigh and started to Canada after my brother Joseph, taking my brother-in-law, John P. Greene, who was then on his way to his circuit, preaching the Methodist doctrine. . . . After finding my brother Joseph, and explaining to him what I had learned of the Gospel in its purity, his heart rejoiced, and he returned home with me, where we arrived in March.[23]

Soon after Brigham and Joseph arrived back in Mendon, John, Sr., Phinehas, and Joseph hitched up and left, once again for Columbia, where father John and Joseph "both became convinced of the truth of Mormonism" and all three asked to be baptized. Phinehas and his father were baptized the next day (April 5, 1832) and Joseph was baptized the day following (the second anniversary of the founding of the church). The three jubilantly headed back to Mendon on April 7.[24] Phinehas's account of his, father John's, and Joseph's baptisms supplies some corroboration to Heber Kimball's linking the missionaries with Pennsylvania in that it states that both John, Sr. and Joseph were baptized in Columbia by Daniel Bowen, presumably the same Daniel Bowen named by Heber as being among the missionaries.[25]

It is also interesting to reflect on why Brigham did not accompany his father and two brothers on the eventful second trip to Pennsylvania. On this, however, the record is silent. Whatever may have been his reasons, Brigham did not hesitate long in following the example of his father and brothers. He was baptized within four or five days of their return as new members of the "Church of Christ."

> April 14th, 1832, I was baptized by Eleazer Miller, who confirmed me at the water's edge. We returned home, about two miles, the weather being cold and snowy; and before my clothes were dry on my back he laid his hands on me and ordained me an Elder, at which I marvelled. According to the words of the Savior, I felt a humble, child-like spirit, witnessing unto me that my sins were forgiven.[26]

Brigham may have "marvelled" at being thrust into a position of authority (his ordination as an elder) before his clothes were dry, but he wasted no time in becoming a totally dedicated "servant of the Lord." His discourses and writings reflect a strong testimony from the beginning—a conversion of the heart and mind as well as of the spirit. Despite the trials and tribulations suffered by early members of the church, Brigham steadfastly testified of the truth of the gospel of Jesus Christ, restored through the instrumentality of Joseph

Smith, a modern prophet of God, whom Brigham loved, honored, and staunchly defended throughout the remainder of Smith's life, and beyond.

In quick succession the rest of the John Young family entered the waters of baptism—Fanny, Rhoda, Susannah, Lorenzo, and Louisa, with their husbands and families, in 1832; John, Jr. and Nancy in 1833. Additionally, "many of my cousins, uncles, and other classes of what we call relatives" also joined the church.[27] Brigham's wife Miriam accepted baptism soon after her husband—with no prompting whatever from him. Regarding her decision, Brigham stated, "I did not know, when I was baptized, whether my wife believed the Gospel or not. . . . I did not ask my wife whether she believed the Gospel; I did not ask her whether she would be baptized. Faith, repentance, and baptism are free for all."[28] Brigham also recalled that "in her expiring moments [four months later] she clapped her hands and praised the Lord, and called upon brother Kimball and all around to praise the Lord."[29]

Little is known of the conversions of the numerous other members of the John Young, Sr. family. Brigham gave information on the conversions of only his father and brothers Phinehas, Joseph, and Lorenzo. Of Lorenzo he stated, somewhat superficially, that "in 1832, while residing in Hector . . . , having heard of the Latter-day work, he borrowed a Book of Mormon from a neighbor, and having carefully perused it, became convinced of its truth; whereupon he gathered up his effects, and took his family, and started for Jackson county. . . . He tarried a few weeks in . . . Mendon, . . . during which time he further became confirmed in the Latter-day work."[30] Of John, Jr. it is recorded that he was baptized by his brother Joseph.[31]

By 1832 the Mendon branch of the Church of Christ, swelled more than double by members of the John Young, Sr. family, might have been considered to be "thriving." Its membership, including unbaptized children, numbered at least fifty-eight if the below record is accurate.[32]

*Mendon Branch*

*Organized Spring 1832*

*Members*

John Young Sr. & wife, Hannah
Edward Young
Brigham Young & wife, Miriam & 2 daughters
Phinehas H. Young, his wife, Clarissa & 5 children
Louisa, her husband, Joel H. Sanford, & 5 children
Rhoda, her husband, John P. Greene, & 7 children
Susannah, her husband, William B. Stilson, and 4 children
Fanny, her husband, Roswell Murray
Joseph Young
Heber C. Kimball, his wife, Vilate (Fanny's daughter), and
    2 children
Ira Bond & his wife, Charlotte
Rufus Parks
John Morton & his wife, Betsey
Nathan Tomlinson & wife
Israel Barlow
Annis Barlow (Israel's mother)
Johathan Barlow (Israel's brother)
Truman Barlow (Israel's brother)
George Lockwood (Israel Barlow's half brother)
Anis Lockwood (George's sister)
Rhoda Lockwood (George's sister)
Julie Ann Lockwood (George's half sister)

That the members of this new branch were dedicated (as well as poor) is indicated by a comment made by Heber Kimball several years later.

> Women would come from Victor, a distance of three miles, to the town of Mendon, New York, where I lived; and I have seen them walk barefooted until they came near where I lived, and then they would put on their white stockings and shoes to go into meeting; and when they came out of meeting and had passed off a little out of sight, they would pull off their shoes and stockings and go home barefooted, for the purpose of saving their fine shoes and stockings which they had spun and knit out of flax.[33]

The enthusiasm of these women was apparently supported by the enthusiasm of such as John Young, Sr., Brigham, Joseph, and Heber Kimball, who, while gathering wood one day,

> were pondering upon those things which had been told us by the Elders, and upon the saints gathering in Zion, when the glory of God shone upon us, and we saw the gathering of the saints to Zion, and the glory that would rest upon them; and many more things connected with that great event, such as the sufferings and persecutions that would come upon the people of God, and the calamities and judgments that would come upon the world. These things caused such great joy to spring up in our bosoms that we were hardly able to contain ourselves, and we did shout aloud "Hosannah to God and the Lamb."[34]

The reaction to members of the new Mendon branch by other New Yorkers was typical. They were curious, and in most cases they were incensed.[35] Those particularly incensed by the formation and activity of the branch were the faithful of the town's Baptist church, who had to suffer the indignity of having some of their membership (the Heber C. Kimballs, for example) renounce their allegiance to become Mormons. The Methodists most probably were also upset when the John Young, Sr. family, Methodists all, crossed over.

The *Wayne Sentinel*, a Palmyra newspaper, carried a small item on April 18, 1832 (four days after Brigham was baptized) regarding the branch.

> A Rochester paper mentions that Mormonism has "taken root" in a certain church in the town of Mendon, Monroe county. The preacher says he shall never die, but be translated, after the manner of Enoch, and that in eighteen months Mormonism will be the prevailing religion; and that in five years, the wicked are to be swept from the face of the earth.[36]

Records of the Mendon Baptist Church indicate that several of its members were excluded "for imbibing the heresy of Mormonism. . . . A portion of the Church protested against measures that were adopted in Protracted Meetings, maintaining that such measures had a tendency to bring persons into the Church, whose conversion was of the passions, and not of the heart."[37]

Hiram K. Stimson, an old-time Mendon resident who later became a well-known Baptist minister, recalled that at one meeting a large group of people had assembled to hear the words of Brigham Young and Heber C. Kimball. Stimson said that Brigham had left the Methodists and belonged to what were called the Giffordites (named for Mormon missionary Alpheus Gifford) and that Brigham

> was quite fervent, and spoke with much feeling and effect. He was regarded as stronger in heart than in head. His faith and piety were counted for more force than his intellect. Heber C. Kimball, on the other hand, was respected as a man of much more mental power, but not of great devotion in comparison with his associate, Young.[38]

Interestingly, for the next several years the Mendon Baptist Church experienced little peace. "In reviewing the history of this Church," stated one report,

> we learn she has passed through a variety of seasons. Like a vessel at sea, she has experienced dark stormy nights and days of sun-light. . . . The Church has been troubled with Mormonism, Millerism and Extraordinary Spiritualism.[39]

Of these Baptists, Brigham once said (with considerable sarcasm):

> In the Branch where I lived, we had not met together three times before our beloved, kind, anti-Godlike Baptist priests and people declared that we made a practice of meeting together, stripping stark naked, and there having the "holy roll." . . . In a very thort time we were all thieves in the estimation of our so-called Christian neighbors.[40]

As could be expected, much of a negative nature to endure on the record in later years was directed at Brigham

Young personally. One *Ontario Republican Times* (Canandaigua) story, after praising him for the tenderness he showed his wife, stated that

> We did not take up our pen to defend Brigham Young as he is, but Brigham Young as he was, while he lived in Canandaigua, before he became a Mormon. . . . We never thought him fanatical, until after he became a Mormon; he was looked upon by his neighbors generally to be a consistent Christian.[41]

Another *Republican Times* article, quoting from a letter submitted by Alonzo Beebe, described Brigham as a loud-mouthed religious fanatic who frequently held meetings in old uninhabited log houses and barns, "always yelling and shouting at the top of his voice when speaking to his hearers."[42] Brigham read this 1857 clipping and responded to the paper by letter, charging that Beebe "relies on his fancy for his arguments, and his imagination for his facts."

> I never held meetings in partnerships with any person, nor ever preached, or pretended to, while I lived in the town of Canandaigua, nor ever spoke in meeting, except once, in a prayer meeting, in the house I lived in, when probably I occupied from two to five minutes. There is a possibility of my having spoken in prayer meetings at other times, but I have no recollection of it. If I had, I think I would have remembered it, for I found myself materially frightened when I found myself in the meeting I have mentioned.[43]

## CHAPTER SIX

# Brigham Young, Missionary

*"I wanted to thunder and roar out the
Gospel to the nations."*
   Brigham Young
   Sermon of February 29, 1863
   *Journal of Discourses* 1: 313-14

B righam Young's conversion to Mormonism was full and
wholehearted. Although it was never required of him,
he vowed that he could have forsaken all his friends and
family to embrace the gospel. "I felt, yes, I can leave my father,
my brothers and sisters, and my wife and children, if they will
not serve the Lord and go with me."[1] And, indeed, he spent
the summer of 1832 "preaching the Gospel in the regions
around about, baptizing and raising up churches."[2] He
journeyed to many places in western New York, holding
meetings in homes and schoolhouses and baptizing many.
Among the communities noted in his journal and in other
accounts are Reading, Hornby, Hector, Avon, and Warsaw
and Canandaigua—all places familiar to those acquainted
with western New York.[3]

He was well aware of his lack of education and his
inexperience as an exhorter, but he strived hard to improve
himself. He once stated that

> had it not been that I clearly saw and understood that the
> Lord Almighty would take the weak things of this world
> to confound the mighty, the wise, and the talented, there
> was nothing that could have induced me or persuaded
> me to have ever become a public speaker.[4]

Of his missionary zeal, Brigham recounted that

> It burned in my bones like fire pent up, so I [commenced] to preach the Gospel of life to the people. . . . Nothing would satisfy me but to cry abroad to the world, what the Lord was doing in the latter days. . . . I had to go out and preach, lest my bones should consume within me.[5]

"For me to travel and preach without purse or scrip, was never hard," Brigham would say. Apparently he possessed more than mere zeal. Inexperienced in public speaking though he might have been, he also admitted to a sensitivity not exhibited by others.

> I never saw the day, I never was in the place, nor went into a house, when I was alone, or when I would take the lead and do the talking, but what I could get all I wanted. Though I have been with those who would take the lead and be mouth, and been turned out of doors a great many times, and could not get a night's lodging. But when I was mouth I never was turned out of doors; I could make the acquaintance of the family, and sit and sing to them and chat with them, and they would feel friendly towards me; and when they learned that I was a "Mormon" Elder it was after I had gained their good feelings.[6]

In the fall of 1832 Brigham, his brother Joseph, and Heber C. Kimball decided to travel to Kirtland, Ohio, to visit the Prophet Joseph Smith. Brigham wrote, "We visited many friends on the way, and some branches of the Church. We exhorted them and prayed with them, and I spoke in tongues. Some pronounced it genuine and from the Lord, and others pronounced it of the Devil."[7]

Arriving at Kirtland, Brigham and Heber first visited the John P. Greenes, who had just arrived from New York. The three travelers rested for a few minutes, took some refreshment, and then started off to see Joseph Smith. Said Brigham,

We went to his father's house, and learned that he was in the woods, chopping. We immediately repaired to the woods, where we found the Prophet, and two or three of his brothers, chopping and hauling wood.

Here my joy was full at the privilege of shaking the hand of the Prophet of God, and received the sure testimony, by the Spirit of prophecy, that he was all that any man could believe him to be, as a true Prophet. He was happy to see us, and bid us welcome. We soon returned to his house, he accompanying us.[8]

Joseph Young recalled that after introductions had been made Smith said, "Brethren, I am glad to see you."

At this he threw down his ax, and said, "Boys take care of my ax." And we went with him to his house. He introduced us to his wife Emma; who was in bed with the infant, Joseph, her first born. This was in November, 1832 [Brigham stated it was in September]. We tarried there seven days; and then took leave of the man that could reveal the hidden things and the mysteries of the kingdom of God, as no other man ever did before.[9]

The first evening after their arrival, Brigham again spoke in tongues, then reported a prophetic statement that Joseph Smith (Brigham was told) made to others at the time, a statement that when it came true was to have a great and permanent impact on the church.

As soon as we arose from our knees the brethren flocked around him [Joseph Smith] and asked him his opinion concerning the gift of tongues that was upon me. He told them it was of the pure Adamic language. . . . "It is of God, and *the time will come when Brother Brigham Young will preside over this church.*"[10]

Following their week's stay in Kirtland, Brigham, his brother Joseph, and Heber returned to Mendon, where they remained about two months. Consumed with the desire to preach the gospel, Brigham and his brother Joseph set out for Kingston, Ontario, in December, walking "most of the way through snow and mud from one to two feet deep."[11]

In February they returned to Mendon after crossing Lake Ontario from Kingston on the ice. Brigham continued his residence with Heber C. Kimball and spent much of his time preaching in the neighboring country. In the spring Brigham and Joseph left for Canada, again on foot, organizing a branch of the church in nearby Lyons on their way. They stopped to preach in several communities in northern New York, among them Theresa, Indian River Falls, and Ogdensburgh, before they reentered Canada.

After nearly three months of missionary work in Canada, in July Brigham "gathered up the families of brother [James] Lake and son [of Earnestown, Ontario] and started for Kirtland, accompanied by Brothers Daniel and Abraham Wood. After tarrying some time enjoying the society of the Prophet and assisting to locate brother Lake and family, I returned to Mendon."[12] He did not stay long.

By mid-1831 the rapidly expanding church, then called the Church of Jesus Christ, had essentially left New York behind—this before any of the John Young family had joined. "Headquarters" of the church shifted to Kirtland, Ohio when Joseph Smith removed to that town from Fayette, New York, in January 1831. Upon conversion en masse by the John Youngs in 1832, and following Brigham's visit to the prophet in the fall of 1832, the Young "clan" ended their three-year sojourn in and around Mendon and, family by family, moved west. The John Greenes were first (some time prior to Brigham's visit to Kirtland in fall 1832), apparently followed by John, Sr. in the spring of 1833. According to a Monroe County, New York, deed, John, Sr. sold forty-five acres of land (to Rufus Richardson for $725.30) on May 14, 1833. (Later, John filed an affidavit with the War Department stating that he had removed to Kirtland in June 1833).[13]

John's wife, Hannah, refused to accompany him and instead went to live with one of her sons (by a previous marriage) in Tyrone. After John had lived in Kirtland for nearly two years, she wrote to him and said that if he would come for her, she would live with him again. So Lorenzo, accompanied by John, traveled to New York, packed up Hannah, and returned to Kirtland. There John and Hannah lived in fairly comfortable circumstances until the time came for the Saints to evacuate Kirtland. Once again Hannah refused to establish herself anew in a strange place. According to family tradition she returned to New York, where she lived with son Edward (and perhaps other members of her family) until her death.[14]

Of the early Kirtland days, Brigham said:

> If any man that ever did gather with the Saints was any poorer than I was—it was because he had nothing. I had something and I had nothing; if he had less than I had, I do not know what it could be. I had two children to take care of—that was all. I was a widower. "Brother Brigham, had you any shoes?" No; not a shoe to my foot, except a pair of borrowed boots. I had no winter clothing, except a homemade coat that I had had three or four years. "Any pantaloons?" No. "What did you do? Did you go without?" No; I borrowed a pair to wear till I could get another pair. I had travelled and preached and given away every dollar of my property. I was worth a little property when I started to preach; but I was something like Bunyan—it was "life, life, eternal life," with me, everything else was secondary. I had travelled and preached until I had nothing left to gather with.[15]

Brigham was to return to New York State on at least four occasions as a missionary. Sustained as one of the original Quorum of Twelve Apostles of the church in 1835, Brigham had thereby become a "special [witness] of the name of Christ in all the world."[16] He had also married Mary Ann Angell. Mary Ann looked after Miriam's children and began to raise her own family.

Brigham's first full-fledged mission as a "special witness" was in the spring of 1836. Accompanied by his brother Joseph, Brigham traveled through New York and New England, visiting relatives and preaching the gospel to them and to all who would listen; many believed and were baptized.[17]

We started from Kirtland, stopped at Providence, R. I., tarried a short time and preached to the saints and others who came to hear us; then proceeded on our journey through Rhode Island, Connecticut, the west part of Massachusetts and New York, and preached by the way, arriving at Kirtland the latter part of September.[18]

On March 13, 1837, Brigham again left Kirtland, on this occasion with Willard Richards, for the eastern states on a special mission assigned them by Joseph Smith. They traveled by stagecoach through Ohio and Pennsylvania to New York. Brigham wrote an interesting account of that mission:

Riding day and night over very rough roads, we became very weary, and tarried a short time to rest ourselves, then took stage coach again, and traveled as far as Canandaigua, where we stopped two nights and one day. While here I visited Martin Harris.

Proceeding on our journey, we rode day and night till we arrived in Albany. Visited Troy, where we transacted considerable business. I purchased from a gentleman there a fine tavern establishment, which was situated in Auburn, directly across the street from the gate of the Penitentiary, which property I still own.

We travelled day and night until we arrived at West Stockbridge, Berkshire Co., Mass., [at] the Dr.'s [i.e., Richards's] old homestead, which he had left the year before. We stayed with Father Richards and family a short time, then proceeded to New Haven, and from thence to New York City, where we stopped a day or two, and took steamboat for Boston by way of Providence, visiting the brethren in Lynn and Salem, also many of the friends and brethren in the country; transacted much business and returned to Berkshire county. My cousin Phinehas Richards and his son George started with me for Kirtland, leaving the Dr. with his friends.

On my return, near Utica, I left the canal and visited my friends in Madison county. Here I found my cousin Hepzibah Richards, who accompanied us by canal as far as Buffalo, where I left my cousins Phinehas and Hepzibah, and a few other friends whom I had gathered up by the way. The ice being still on the lake, steamboats were laid up, but I proceeded by stage to Kirtland, and arrived the latter part of May.[19]

(Why he bought a tavern in Auburn, and how he acquired the money for the purchase, is not known.)

Brigham's next trip east started late in July 1837. On this short mission he was accompanied as far as Buffalo by Joseph Smith, his brother Hyrum, David W. Patten, and Thomas B. Marsh, who were on their way to Canada. Parting company with the others at Buffalo, Brigham took a train to Lockport and from there a line boat on the Erie Canal to Utica, accompanied by his cousin, A. P. Rockwood. "Brother Rockwood stopped at Auburn to see some of our relatives, and I took the cars for Albany."[20] Brigham traveled on to West Stockbridge and arrived by stage at the home of his uncle, Joseph Richards, on August 1, 1837. Later he returned to Albany and took a steamboat to New York, where he remained for several days before returning home to Kirtland.

Brigham's final trip to New York was in 1839, as a stopover on his mission to Great Britain. On July 8, 1838, Joseph Smith had announced a revelation that the twelve apostles must leave Far West, Missouri, on April 26, 1839, to "go over the great waters, and there promulgate my gospel, the fulness thereof, and bear record of my name."[21] After removing his family to Montrose, Iowa, across the Mississippi from Nauvoo, Illinois, the new gathering place of the Mormons, Brigham and other members of the Twelve prepared to leave their families that fall. Brigham was delayed "by a general siege of sickness which swept over the entire community" in the form of malaria from the wetlands along the Mississippi where the Saints had settled. Although stricken with "chills and fever," Brigham was determined to leave.

> My health was so poor I was unable to go thirty rods to the river without assistance. After I had crossed the river I got Israel Barlow to carry me on his horse behind him to Heber C. Kimball's, where I remained sick till the 18th. I left my wife [Mary Ann] sick with a babe only ten days old, and all of my children sick and unable to wait upon each other.[22]

All the clothing Brigham had at the time was what he was wearing. He had made a cap "out of a pair of old pantaloons. I had not even an overcoat. I took a small quilt from the trundle and that served for my overcoat while I was traveling to the state of New York where I had a coarse satinette overcoat given to me.[23] Physically and materially, Brigham was at the bottom rung. But eventually he and the Twelve made their way eastward, assisted by friends, relatives, and "Good Samaritans." At Kirtland the missionaries enjoyed a pleasant visit, and Brigham visited his brother Joseph and his sister Nancy Kent, who had since moved there.

On November 26, 1839, the group departed aboard the steamboat *Columbus*, arriving in Buffalo the next morning. But their troubles were far from over. Brigham wrote in his journal,"We took passages on the stage, (on the 17th) but found our Ohio money would not pass current, and we had to go to a broker's and exchange for Buffalo money by paying a heavy discount." (The entire nation was still experiencing one of the most severe depressions in its history at the time.)[24]

"On arriving at Batavia," Brigham wrote, "we put up at the Genesee House, dedicated our room to the Lord, and had a prayer meeting, asking the Lord to open up our way. . . . We [then] took the cars for Rochester. Elder Kimball left us at Byron [a village between Batavia and Rochester] to visit his friends."[25] Arriving at Rochester, they took the stage and rode through the night to Auburn [a distance of over sixty miles], arriving at 10:00 A.M. Here two of the elders, John Taylor and Theodore Turley, proceeded to New York, "being short of means." Brigham and his remaining companion, George A. Smith, "concluded to stop and preach until the Lord should open the way." They visited Brigham's cousin, George Brigham, who listened attentively to their teachings. "He took us to a hotel, where we slept in a damp room and took additional cold. . . . We walked to Moravia, and found brother Isaac C. Haight and a small Branch of the Church, which had recently been built up in that neighborhood. I preached several times. Brother George A's lungs were so bad he could not preach."[26] Mrs. Mary Helen Grant, daughter of

William Van Orden, one of the early Moravia converts, said years later:

> I remember Brigham Young and George A. Smith being at father's as they were on their way to England. Brigham was very sick there for a week or more. George A. Smith did not have an overcoat and it was very cold weather. He had a piece of patchwork quilt folded cornerwise and wrapped around his shoulders. Father had some "full cloth" as they called it, homemade of course, and he had two young ladies, tailoresses, Mary and Abigail Thorn, come to the house and make an overcoat for him.[27]

From Moravia, Brigham and George A. traveled (on December 7) to visit the Saints in Hamilton. They found them in confusion.

> They had the gift of tongues among them, and the interpretation, and they were so ignorant of the nature of these gifts that they supposed that everything which was spoken in tongues was immediate revelation from God; a false spirit had therefore crept in, and division was the result.
> I taught them that when they spoke in tongues the language might be from the Lord, but with that tongue they spoke the things which were in their hearts, whether they were good or evil; the gift of tongues was given for a blessing to the Saints, but not to govern them nor to control the Elders, or dictate the affairs of the Church. God had placed in the Church different gifts; among which were Apostles, Prophets, helps and governments, and wisdom was profitable to direct.[28]

Before Brigham left, the Saints in Hamilton came to understand these matters. "The brethren were very kind to us," Brigham said; "Brother Benager Moon gave me satinette to make me an overcoat; sister Lucetta Murdock made it for me; this was a great blessing to me, as I had worn a quilt, with a comforter run through it, in lieu of an overcoat, all the way from Nauvoo, which had not much of a ministerial appearance. Held meetings on Tuesday and Thursday evenings."[29]

On Sunday, December 15, Brigham preached in Waterville at Brother Gifford's and returned to Hamilton Monday.

He went to nearby Eaton on December 20 to visit his cousins, Fitch and Salmon Brigham. The following day he returned to Hamilton and called on another cousin, Phinehas Brigham. Phinehas asked several questions about the Prophet Joseph Smith. Brigham recorded:

> I preached the Gospel to him so plainly that he could not make any reply, but had to acknowledge that what I taught was Scriptural and reasonable, and he could not gainsay it; but being a very staunch Baptist and a deacon too, he regretted very much his son was not there, who was educated for a Baptist priest. He thought if his son was there he might be able to enlighten my mind and point out my errors, although he was not able to do it himself.
>
> We had not conversed an hour before his son, the priest, came in, to whom he introduced me, and then sat down with a great deal of composure, believing the son would be able to rebut the doctrine I had advanced.
>
> The son, with all the solemnity and air of a priest, commenced to ask questions. I answered them, and, in return, asked him a few questions, giving him the liberty to rebut any statement I had made by bringing Scripture testimony, as I had read my doctrine from the Bible; but he could not give me any light, neither could he answer the questions I asked him and he was too much of a gentleman—young and inexperienced—to commence a tirade of abuse, as older priests generally did on the character of Joseph Smith and the Book of Mormon, consequently he sat mute as a stock.
>
> I continued my visit with the family for a short time, and when I was about to leave I told them that Baptistism, Methodism, Presbyterianism, Quakerism,Shakerism, and every other ism I had studied and learned, for I desired to know the truth, and found I could put all their doctrines, when simmered down to truth, into a snuff-box of the smallest class, put it into my vest pocket and go my way; but when I found "Mormonism," I found that it was higher than I could reach with my researches, deeper than I was capable of comprehending, and calculated to expand the mind and lead mankind from truth to truth, from light to light, from grace to grace, and exalt him in the celestial kingdom, to become associated with the Gods and the angels. I bade them good night, and went over the hill to Hamilton, and staid at brother Murdoch's.[30]

Brigham remained in the area for three weeks while George A. recuperated from a bout of illness. On January 1, 1840, the two were taken by sleigh to James Gifford's house, where they spent the night. The following day they went by sleigh to Utica, where they boarded a train for Albany. Their missionary travels took them through Massachusetts and Connecticut, and they finally arrived in New York on January 30. The journey had taken about four-and-a-half months.[31]

Brigham and the other members of the Twelve were practically penniless when they arrived in New York City, and consequently they remained there until March to replenish their finances. Finally, on March 9 they sailed for Liverpool, England, aboard the ship *Patrick Henry*. They remained in England for just over one year, returning to New York City (aboard the *Rochester*) in May 1841, collectively having completed a tremendously successful mission that was to result in doubling the membership of the church. Brigham returned to Illinois (via Pittsburgh, the Ohio River, and Cincinnati, arriving in Nauvoo on July 1, 1841, "cordially welcomed by the Prophet Joseph, our families and the saints."[32] He never again saw New York.

# Brigham Young and the New York Experience

The relationship between Brigham Young and New York was reciprocal. From what is known of Brigham Young's later life, his experiences in New York had a significant impact on his character and career. At the same time, after he had become famous, people in New York remembered Brigham and his accomplishments in their state.

Brigham Young's early life was one of hardship and privation. Largely for economic reasons it was necessary for his family to move several times. Frequent illness and financial hardship dogged their footsteps. In his later life, Brigham Young was able to draw upon these early experiences in his sermons and writings to provide lessons for Church members and others whom he met.

Conditions in his early life made hard work a necessity. Currently available evidence indicates that the attitudes he learned in New York carried throughout his life. They included pride in his work, diligence in completing jobs, and personal accountability.

Brigham Young was clearly a product of the New England lower class. At times, his poverty made it impossible to pay his debts. However, after he had become wealthy, his strong sense of honesty, which trait he also developed as a youth in New York, led him whenever possible to pay those debts, in some instances as much as three decades later.

It is clear that Young's early life and experiences in New York dramatically shaped his character and attitudes. He disliked the strict prohibitions of his Methodist parents on such recreational experiences as dancing, reading, and music, and his rebellion against those strictures may have helped to shape his later attitudes which were decidedly favorable to such things. The years of hard physical labor toughened him and strongly influenced his tough attitude toward those he felt were unwilling to work equally as hard. On the other hand, the strict moral training of his youth provided a strong underpinning for his attitudes toward breaches of personal morality. It is also clear that hardship, hard work, and unwavering moralility went far in developing, him into the very capable, though iron-willed and often formidable, leader he ultimately became.

The New York experience also was instrumental in shaping Brigham Young's religious outlook. Central to his life was a religious culture in which the Bible played an important part. His attitude emphasizing Biblical literalism is evident from his insistence that he be baptized by immersion. Undoubtedly, the Bible was the standard by which he measured the doctrines contained in the Book of Mormon, which eventually converted him to Mormonism. This biblical culture, which he shared in abundance with his parents, brothers, and sisters, inculcated a desire for apocalyptic and charismatic experiences which he found in early Mormonism.

It is evident that the relationship between Brigham Young and New Yorkers was reciprocal. After Brigham Young had become famous, people in the Empire State were proud to have a "Brigham Young mantelpiece" or a "Brigham Young chair" in their possession. This pride may have carried so far that items not actually made by the Mormon Prophet were attributed to him. In addition, his neighbors generally remembered him as energetic and capable.

On the whole, the New York years were decisive in molding Brigham Young. His basic attitudes, his sense of commitment, and his strength of character were all in large measure products of his New York experience.

# Notes

Sources are cited in full only once—where they first appear. However, quick reference to the full citation is provided by the use of the *supra* signal. That is, when a source is cited subsequently, the author's last name and/or an abbreviated title is followed by the volume and/or page number of the source, the word *supra,* and the chapter and/or note in this volume where the full citation can be found. For example, a note reading "*JD,* 4:104, *supra,* chap. 1, n. 4" is the abbreviated citation of *Journal of Discourses,* volume 4, page 104, the full citation for which can be found at note 4 of chapter 1 in this volume.

## Chapter 1

1. Regarding John Young and his ancestry, the following is quoted from B. H. Roberts, *A Comprehensive History of the Church of Jesus Christ of Latter-day Saints,* 6 vols. (Provo, Utah: Brigham Young University Press, 1977), p. 287.

> Brigham Young came of an honorable ancestry. His great-grandfather, William Young, was among the original proprietors of Barrington and Nottingham, New Hampshire; where he is first heard of in 1721. "These towns were settled by men, or the children of men, who had shown faithfulness and bravery in the Indian wars. The lands were given to them by the government in recognition of this service. Wm. Young had a number of free-holds in these towns, and bought several other. * * * He resided in later years in Boston, but died in Hopkinton, Massachusetts. In his will in Middlesex County Record he leaves about $10,000.00 to his wife and daughter and minor son and names Rev. S. Barrett as the guardian of the latter." (From Genealogical Chart, Brigham Young Family. See also *History of Brigham Young, Millennial Star,* vol. xxv, pp. 295-6; 310-311; and 326-28 et seq.)
>
> Brigham Young's grandfather, Joseph Young, was a physician and surgeon in the French and Indian War, and was accidentally killed when about forty years of age. Brigham's father, John Young, was born in Hopkinton, Middlesex County, Massachusetts, in [March 7] 1763. . . . At sixteen he enlisted in the American Revolutionary War, and served under General Washington through three campaigns in Massachusetts and New Jersey.

2. James A. Little, "Historical Items about Brigham Young," 2:2, Archives of the Church of Jesus Christ of Latter-day Saints, Salt Lake City (hereafter referred to as Church Archives).

3. Brigham Young, "History of Brigham Young," presented serially in *Latter-day Saints' Millennial Star*, 132 vols. (Manchester and Liverpool: Latter-day Saint Book Depot, 1840-1870), 25:295 (hereafter referred to as HBY).

4. Brigham Young, remarks of October 5, 1856, in *Journal of Discourses*, 26 vols. (Liverpool, England: Latter-day Saints Book Depot, 1854-1886), 4:112 (hereafter referred to as *JD*).

5. Little, "Historical Items about Brigham Young," 2:6, *supra*, n. 2.

6. John Young married Abigail (often referred to as Nabby) Howe in 1785. Abigail Howe was born on August 6, 1766, in Hopkinton, Massachusetts. John and Abigail had eleven children: Nancy, born August 6, 1786, in Hopkinton; Fanny, born November 8, 1787, in Hopkinton; Rhoda, born September 10, 1789, in Platauva District, New York; John, Jr., born May 22, 1791, in Hopkinton; Nabby, born April 23, 1793, in Hopkinton; Susannah, born June 7, 1795, in Hopkinton; Joseph, born April 7, 1787 in Hopkinton; Phinehas Howe, born February 16, 1799, in Hopkinton; Brigham, born June 1, 1801, in Whitingham, Vermont; Louisa, born September 25, 1804, in Sherburne, New York; and Lorenzo Dow, born October 19, 1807, in Sherburne.

7. "Whitingham Deeds," p. 675, recorded November 18, 1800, microfilm record in Genealogical Society Archives, Church of Jesus Christ of Latter-day Saints, Salt Lake City. The property was deeded back to Joseph Mosely in 1802. Ibid., p. 821, recorded December 24, 1802.

8. HBY, 25:295, *supra*, n. 3. For a nearly identical statement, see ibid., p. 423.

9. Franklin Wheeler Young, "Young Family Genealogy," p. 13, Church Archives, *supra*, n. 2. Frequent political subdivisions of New York towns were made as their populations increased. On March 25, 1808, the section of Sherburne in which the Youngs lived became known as Stafford. Twelve days later, however, the name was changed to Smyrna. See Franklin B. Hough, *Gazetteer of the State of New York* (Albany, 1872), p. 224. The present-day towns of Smyrna and Sherburne are on either side of the Chenango River, their centers four miles apart.

10. See also Communication to the *Chenango Union* (Norwich, N. Y.), May 8, 1883, in Lathrop Scrapbook, pp. 66-67, in Sherburne Public Library, Sherburne, N. Y.

11. Correspondence with Mrs. Vaughn Fargo, Smyrna, N. Y., town historian.

12. Lathrop Scrapbook, p. 59, *supra*, n. 10.

13. At least one shred of evidence indicates that the Youngs lived near Lansingville at the time. The late Clarence Jefferson wrote that Brigham lived with his parents on the shore of Cayuga Lake, near Lansing Station, and that he attended Drake schoolhouse. HBY, 24:423, *supra*, n. 3. See also sources cited in note 16 below.

14. Susa Young Gates, "Notes on the Young and Howe Families," *Utah Genealogical and Historical Magazine* 11 (January 1920):182-83.

15. James A. Little, "Biography of Lorenzo Dow Young," *Utah Historical Quarterly*, 14 (1946):25.

16. See Isabelle H. Parish, "Cemeteries in the Town of Lansing," DeWitt Historical Society, Ithaca, N. Y., pp. 60-61. See also *History of Tioga, Cheming, Tomkins and Schuyler Counties* (Philadelphia, 1879) (hereafter referred to as *Four-County History*), p. 520, which states in part: "The cemetery adjoining J. W. Hamilton's farm was connected with the Methodist Episcopal Church. Brigham Young's mother is said to be buried here; but, if so, no stone marks the spot." Another account, in the *New York Times*, September 16, 1877, reported that a Dr. J. P. Barnum of Louisville, Kentucky, who was raised in the same area as the Youngs near Lansing, also claimed to have seen Abigail's grave near Lansingville, though the doctor was not born when Brigham left that country and went west. He said that Mrs. Young died when Brigham was about fifteen years of age and that he had often seen her grave, which was situated on Ben Wegger's farm near Lansing, and only a few miles from his home.

17. Brigham Young, discourse of August 15, 1852, in *JD*, 6:290, *supra*, n. 4.

18. *New York Times*, September 16, 1877.

19. Information supplied by S. Dilworth Young, Salt Lake City. Brigham Young stated that Fanny married Carr when she was sixteen years old, or in 1803 or 1804. See HBY, 25:310, *supra*, n. 3.

20. Little, "Biography of Lorenzo Dow Young," p. 25, *supra*, n. 15. Sugar Hill is a sparsely settled area now encompassing portions of the present towns of Orange and Tyrone in Schuyler County, originally in Steuben County. Much of this area is now a forest preserve and game management area.

21. HBY, 25:310-11, *supra*, n. 3.

22. Little, "Historical Items about Brigham Young," 2:3, *supra*, n. 2.

23. Ibid.

24. A New York map dated 1819 shows no town at the southern tip of Seneca Lake. The place name *Salubria*, perhaps a village, is shown nearby, however.

25. *Four-County History*, p. 664, *supra*, n. 16.

26. Ibid., p. 680. Daniel Kent was married to John Young's oldest daughter, Nancy.

27. Little, "Biography of Lorenzo Dow Young," pp. 25-26, *supra*, n. 15. The account states: "During the winter of 1815 and 1816, Lorenzo's brothers, John, Joseph, Phinehas, and Brigham were chopping timber and clearing land for their father, and as there were no female members of the family, Lorenzo was taken home to cook and assist in the house." The account is suspect, given the fact that Lorenzo was only eight years old in 1815 and that John, Jr. probably lived elsewhere considering the fact that he was married in 1813.

28. John Young Revolutionary War Pension File, W.11908 BLWT 101, 305-160-55, National Archives, Washington, D.C.

29. HBY, 25:295, *supra*, n. 3.

30. Little, "Biography of Lorenzo Dow Young," p. 130, *supra*, n. 15.

31. Ibid.

32. John, Jr., in his old age, said, "Frankly, if you ever write my history, I want you to say of me in all other things, I was fond of hunting." Ibid.

33. Ibid., pp. 130-31.

34. "Syrupy Scenes on Sugar Hill," feature article in *Elmira Sunday Telegram* (N. Y.), March 23, 1947.

35. Brigham Young, discourse of October 8, 1868, in *JD*, 12:278, *supra*, n. 4. Apparently, John Young, in addition to clearing his own land, hired himself out (and his boys as well) to clear and otherwise work the land of others.

36. Brigham Young, discourse of August 8, 1869, ibid., 14:103.

37. Romulus is situated between Cayuga and Seneca lakes, about thirty-four miles from Genoa via Cayuga Bridge. If this account is accurate, the boys may have made such a trip (via Cayuga Bridge) or may have crossed Cayuga Lake by boat somewhere west or northwest of Genoa. See map.

38. Brigham Young, discourse of August 2, 1857, in *JD*, 4:312, *supra*, n. 4.

39. Brigham Young, discourse of April 20, 1856, ibid., 3:320-21.

40. Brigham Young, remarks of June 30, 1867, ibid., 12:95.

41. Brigham Young, discourse of February 6, 1853, ibid., 2:94.

42. Little, "Historical Items about Brigham Young," 2:3, *supra*, n. 2.

43. Brigham Young, remarks of August 2, 1857, in *JD*, 5:97, *supra*, n. 4.

44. Brigham Young, discourse of April 6, 1857, ibid., 4:312.

## Chapter 2

1. Brigham Young, sermon of November 6, 1864, in *JD*, 10:360, *supra*, chap. 1, n. 4. Lorenzo implied another reason for Brigham's departure when he recalled that Brigham remained home until his father married Hannah Brown, then "he again went from home." Little, "Historical Items about Brigham Young," 2:6, *supra*, chap. 1, n. 2.

2. Sylvester J. Matthews. *The Antiquarian* (Auburn, N. Y.), January 18, 1902. This was a tabloid published for a brief period consisting primarily of local history.

3. Ulysses Prentiss Hedrick, *A History of Agriculture in the State of New York* (New York: Hill and Wang, 1933; reprinted, 1966), p. 78.

4. Mathews, *The Antiquarian, supra*, n. 2.

5. Ibid.

6. Little, "Biography of Lorenzo Dow Young," p. 26, *supra*, chap. 1, n. 15; Young, "Young Family Genealogy," p. 13, *supra*, chap. 1, n. 9; and *Auburn Gazette*, November 25, 1818.

7. Henry Hall, *History of Auburn* (Auburn, N. Y., 1869), pp. 121-22.

8. "Biographical Sketch of Brigham Young," manuscript, dated April 18, 1872, in Church Archives, *supra*, chap. 1, n. 2.

9. Brigham Young, discourse of August 31, 1875, in *JD*, 18:76, *supra*, chap. 1, n. 4.

10. Benjamin F. Hall, "Genealogical and Biographical Sketch of the Late Honorable Elijah Miller," p. 80, manuscript, ca. 1877, in Cayuga County Historian's Office, Auburn, N. Y.

11. Brigham may have had at least a speaking acquaintance with Miller's daughter, Frances. Seven years later she married William H. Seward, who was to become governor of New York and secretary of state under Presidents Abraham Lincoln and Andrew Johnson.

On a trip to the Orient in 1869, William Seward stopped off in Salt Lake City to visit Brigham Young. (Both men were about the same age.) After exchanging greetings, Brigham reportedly asked, "Governor Seward, who lives in Squire Brown's house at Auburn now?" Seward replied, "I bought it from Squire Brown, and lived there a year or two, and since then it has had several owners." Brigham then said, "I worked on that house as a journeyman carpenter when they were building it, about the same time that I was employed at the Theological Seminary." Frederick W. Seward, *Seward at Washington, 1861-1872* (New York, 1891).

12. Hall, *History of Auburn*, pp. 380, 383, *supra*, n. 7; and Little, "Historical Items about Brigham Young," 2:2, *supra*, chap. 1, n. 2.

13. Mrs. Jerome Rich (formerly Mary Ann Wadsworth), also suggested that Brigham worked on the construction of the Joseph Wadsworth home. "Joseph Wadsworth built the farmhouse on what was known as the Dunning Farm, and Brigham Young, the Mormon, is supposed to have been the journeyman carpenter as he was then residing in Port Byron."

14. *Auburn Advertiser-Journal*, January 13, 1927. In 1947 the Brown house was demolished and the property is now the site of New York Telephone Company's Auburn office. Dunning further recalled:

> Sometime during the war, about 1862-63, one day a carriage drove up from the city and a gentleman announced himself as John Young, a son of Brigham Young. He was on his return from a trip to Europe and had been requested by his father to stop off at Auburn and find the Wadsworth place and see if any of the Wadsworths were still living there. He was told that my mother, a daughter of Joseph Wadsworth, was living there, and that her father died in 1855. Ibid.

15. Account of death of David M. Dunning and related information supplied by his granddaughter, Mrs. Charlotte Kruger, Auburn, N.Y.; and Mary Van Sickle Wait, *Brigham Young in Cayuga County* (Ithaca, N.Y.: DeWitt Historical Society, 1964), p. 44.

16. Mathews, *The Antiquarian, supra,* n. 2; and Colonel John Richardson of New Hope, Pa., to Mary Van Sickle Wait, January 4, 1965.

17. Dean C. Jessee, *Letters of Brigham Young to His Sons* (Salt Lake City: Deseret Book Co., 1974), p. 23.

18. Brigham Young, discourse of April 20, 1856, in *JD,* 3:323, *supra,* chap. 1, n. 4.

19. Brigham Young to George Hickox, February 19, 1876, Ontario County Historical Society, Canandaigua, N. Y.

20. Brigham Young, sermon of November 6, 1864, in *JD,* 10:360, *supra,* chap. 1, n. 4.

## Chapter 3

1. Mathews, *The Antiquarian,* January 18, 1902, *supra,* chap. 2, n. 2. Port Byron, originally Bucksville, was established on the Erie Canal's "middle section," which had been in operation since the summer of 1820. See E. H. Kerns, *History of Port Byron and Mentz* (Port Byron, N. Y.: Port Byron Chronicle, 1922), p. 5.

2. *Auburn Daily Bulletin,* August 31, 1877.

3. William Hayden, "In the days of Long Ago," *Port Byron Chronicle,* March 5, 1904.

4. Ibid.

5. Ibid. February 17, 1904: David B. Smith to Brigham Young, February 8, 1853, Church Archives, *supra,* chap. 1, n. 2.

6. Cayuga County Deeds, Book Z, pp. 432-34, Cayuga County Courthouse archives, Auburn, N. Y.

7. Accounts of Brigham's employment at the pail factory (and employment in Port Byron proper) are sketchy and are conflicting as to dates. Whether he was first employed at Haydenville, then Port Byron, or vice-versa, cannot be determined with surety. Records indicate that Parks's pail factory was not established until 1828 (see Elliot G. Storke, *History of Cayuga County, New York, 1789-1879* [Philadelphia, 1879], p. 357.), yet William Hayden, many years after the fact and perhaps with considerable embellishments and inaccuracy as to details, recounted that Brigham's employment at the pail factory was instrumental in his being introduced to his wife, Miriam Works, whom he married in 1824, and that his employment in Port Byron came later. (Hayden was born in 1821 and therefore was but a young boy when the events he recounted involving Brigham Young occurred.) See William Hayden, account in *Syracuse Sunday Herald,* February 21, 1904. Still another piece of important evidence is in conflict with at least the Storke account of the pail factory not opening until 1828. Brigham Young stated that he moved to Oswego for a time (he did not say when or for how long), then moved on to Mendon in the spring of 1829, indicating that he left Haydenville in 1828.

8. Hayden, *Syracuse Sunday Herald, supra,* n. 7.

9. Ibid. Hayden reported that Brigham first built a water wheel.

> His wheel had an upright shaft some five or six feet high with a slant of 35 to 40 degrees. On the top was arranged a frame to hold a large old-fashioned dinner pot, into which the paint was put with a cannon ball weighing twenty-five pounds. When the wheel was set in motion, it would revolve in one direction, while its slanting motion would cause the ball to roll in the opposite direction. The idea was that the continued rolling of the ball would grind or pulverize the paint to the desired fineness. This improvement was pronounced by all a complete success and thereafter Brigham was consulted in regard to all proposed alterations and improvements upon the premises.
>
> The cannon ball mentioned was captured from the British at Saratoga in 1777 by Brigham's father, who carried it to his home, more than 100 miles, on foot. Brigham himself brought it from Vermont. He left it with my brother and for many years it was used to grind indigo as it had formerly ground paint. It is now in the possession of my brother, John Hayden.

Again, Hayden's account is inaccurate; for example, Brigham could not have packed the twenty-five pound cannonball from Vermont as he was only one year old at the time.

10. William Hayden, account in *Auburn Daily Advertiser*, February 17, 1904. The somewhat embroidered account reads:

> That Mr. Young was quick to discern and instantly to comprehend a situation was amply illustrated a short time after commencing his work in the factory. The floors of the factory were covered with pine shavings and the only fire protection was numerous pails in each room, filled with water. A thunderstorm had begun and was fast reaching its height. As it had become too dark for work, the machinery was stopped and most of the workmen, with several outsiders, had congregated on the second floor when a most terrific crash came, throwing stove and stove pipe in all directions and filling the room with ashes and dust. Almost as quick as the lightning itself, Brigham caught up two pails of water and started for the lower floor, shouting to the others still standing as if paralyzed; "Every man get a pail of water and watch for fire." His prompt action alone saved the building from destruction. The slight affects of this lightning stroke are still out to those curious to see.

11. Hayden, *Syracuse Sunday Herald, supra*, n. 7.

12. Susa Young Gates, *The Life Story of Brigham Young* (Freeport, N.Y.: Books for Libraries Press, 1971, reprint), p. 19. Gates went on to describe Brigham as "five feet ten in height, vigorous, handsome and magnetic."

13. Storke, *History of Cayuga County*, p. 357, *supra*, n. 7. Half Acre was situated amidst stately maple trees two miles west of Auburn, and in early days was known officially as Aurelius Post Office. Apparently the Half Acre name came from the fact that all three taverns at the crossroads were on less than a half acre of land.

14. *Cayuga Patriot*, November 3, 1824.

15. Letter from Mrs. Webb, *Auburn Bulletin*, September 11, 1877. See also Ann Eliza Webb, *Wife No. 19* (Hartford, Conn., 1875), pp. 468-69. Gilbert Weed had come to the Aurelius area from Saratoga County in eastern New York State about 1800. He, his father of the same name, and their families were prominent Aurelius citizens. Interestingly, Ann Eliza Webb, the daughter of Elizabeth Churchill Webb, became the plural wife of Brigham Young and was to enjoy some notoriety in the 1870s following her divorce from the Mormon leader.

16. *Auburn Bulletin*, August 31, 1877.

17. Interview with Mrs. Marion Knapp. Mrs. Knapp said that the Youngs spent their honeymoon at her home, located about three miles south of Port Byron. She said that for years "Mormons from the West, some of them descendants of Brigham Young" included her home on their itineraries of historical Mormon landmarks. Mrs. Knapp, with much pride, pointed out the upstairs bedroom where it is said that Brigham and Miriam lived during the first months of their marriage while he worked at a factory across the road.

18. Interview with Howard Power.

19. Hayden, *Syracuse Sunday Herald, supra*, n. 7.

20. Susa Young Gates to William Hayden, June 1, 1904, Church Archives, *supra*, chap. 1, n. 2. The letter was in response to his article on Brigham Young reprinted in the *Deseret Evening News*, May 14, 1904.

21. Hayden, *Syracuse Sunday Herald, supra*, n. 7.

22. Hayden, *Auburn Daily Advertiser, supra*, n. 10.

23. Interview with Mrs. Marion Knapp.

24. Hayden, *Syracuse Sunday Herald, supra*, n. 7.

25. Ibid.

26. Ibid.

27. Brigham Young to David B. Smith, June 1, 1853, Church Archives, *supra*, chap. 1, n. 2. Apparently Brigham, in his statement that he built the tannery, meant that he had been employed in his capacity as a carpenter to build or assist in the building of the structure.

28. Hiram McKee to Brigham Young, April 4, 1860, and Brigham Young to Hiram McKee, May 3, 1860, in Brigham Young Papers, Church Archives, *supra*, chap. 1, n. 2.

29. James Little purchased (for $765) nineteen acres of land (on Lot 55) in Aurelius in 1818, where he carried on farming and particularly the production of garden seeds for market. (An 1821 handbill boasts that the "Everlasting Sweet Pea" was also developed on his farm.) He is credited by some to have been the first man in New York State to sell packaged seeds, and with introducing tomatoes for table use in this area. To do this he had to procure a permit from Governor DeWitt Clinton. "Love apples," as tomatoes were then called, were thought to be poisonous and were grown strictly for decorative purposes.

Little frequently visited Auburn to dispose of his produce and bring home supplies. Near the road was a deep hole from which sand had been taken for building purposes. Apparently the bank had caved in after Little had passed it on his way into the village. As he was returning home after dark, the wheels of his wagon slipped into the hole on one side, turning it over and pinning him under the load. He was found dead at the scene the following morning, his horse grazing nearby. The *Cayuga Republican* of Wednesday, November 20, 1822, reported the accident.

> On Friday night last, about eleven o'clock, Mr. James Little, of this town, aged 32, on his way home from this village, in a one horse wagon upset, and fell, together with a bag or two of flour, &c. on to him—he was found in this situation in the morning, dead. He has left a wife and three small children. Mr. Little carried on gardening and raising garden seeds, young fruit trees, &c. on a large scale, and was a very useful man in his calling, in this part of the State.

Little left no will. His brothers-in-law, Joseph and Brigham Young, and a neighbor, Albigence B. Munroe, were appointed (Joseph Young as administrator) to settle the estate. (A document among the estate papers contains the three signatures, including what may be the earliest known autograph of Brigham Young.) See Cayuga County Deeds, Book M-R-W-D, p. 123, *supra*, n. 6; and Harriet F. Little, *Descendants of William Little, Jr., and Allied Families* (Provo, Utah: Brigham Young University Press, 1958), pp. 11, 22.

30. Mendon Branch records, Church Archives, *supra*, chap. 1, n. 2.

31. HBY, 25:423, *supra*, chap. 1, n. 3. See also Lucy Mack Smith, *History of Joseph Smith by His Mother* (Salt Lake City: Bookcraft, 1958), pp. 168-70.

32. Monroe County Deeds, Liber 25, p. 39, Monroe County Clerk's office, Rochester, N.Y. John purchased an additional forty-five acres in 1830. Ibid., Liber 23, p. 542.

33. HBY, 25:423, *supra*, chap. 1, n. 3. The Phinehas Youngs took up residence in Victor, three miles east of Mendon.

34. U.S. Department of Commerce, Bureau of the Census, *Fifth Census, 1830* (Washington, D. C.: U.S. Government Printing Office, 1831).

35. Mr. Munroe's shop was within a mile of Half Acre at a place locally known as "Stony Pitch." Munroe carried on a sizable business and employed several young men as apprentices. After his injury, Lorenzo was under a doctor's care for over two months. He recovered, but he never again worked at the forge. See Little, "Biography of Lorenzo Dow Young," pp. 28-29, *supra*, chap. 1, n. 15; story related by Charles Carter of Aurelius, as told to Donna Reiller, former town supervisor of Aurelius. See also Munroe estate papers, Cayuga County Surrogate Court records, Auburn, N.Y.

36. HBY, 25: *supra*, chap. 1, n. 3.

37. Mendon Branch records, Church Archives. *supra*, chap. 1, n. 2; HBY, 25:375, 407, *supra*, chap. 1, n. 3; and Little, "Historical Items about Brigham Young," p. 2., *supra*, chap. 1, n. 2.

38. HBY, 25:375, 424, *supra*, chap. 1, n. 3.

39. Charles F. Milliken, *The Beginnings of Mormonism* (Rochester, N.Y.: Rochester Historical Society, Publication Fund Series, 1926), 5:42.

40. Anah B. Yates, "The Pioneers of Mendon," in *Honeoye Falls Times*, February 2, 1922.

41. Milliken, *Beginnings of Mormonism*, 5:42, *supra*, n. 39.

42. George Washington Allen, "Brigham Young and Mormonism," pp. 5-6, manuscript in possession of J. Sheldon Fisher, Valentown Museum, Fishers, N.Y.

43. HBY, 25:438, *supra*, chap. 1, n. 3

44. That Brigham and his family moved to Canandaigua in 1830 is substantiated by the fact that the family appears twice in the 1830 U. S. Census—in both Mendon and Canandaigua. Apparently, the family moved while the census was still in process. "Number Nine" refers to the ninth township in the Phelps and Gorham Purchase land development, which at one time comprised some 2.6 million acres. See Hough, *Gazetteer*, p. 51, *supra*, chap. 1, n. 9; and *Fifth Census, 1830*, *supra*, n. 34

45. Brigham Young to an unidentified person, July 23, 1858.

46. Heber C. Kimball, remarks of June 7, 1862, in *JD*, 9:329, *supra*, chap. 1, n. 4.

47. Milliken, *Beginnings of Mormonism*, 5:42, *supra*, n. 39; and Reverend J. Willard Webb, "A Memorial Sermon—The Life and Character of George Hickox," undated, Brigham Young Collection, Church Archives, *supra*, chap. 1, n. 2.

48. University of Rochester Library archives, Rochester, N.Y.

49. Hayden, *Syracuse Sunday Herald*, *supra*, n. 7.

50. Brigham Young to John W. Young, February 7, 1866, Church Archives, *supra*, chap. 1, n. 2.

51. *Auburn Advertiser Union*, March 19, 1866. Note the sarcasm of the parenthetical.

52. Storke, *History of Cayuga County*, pp. 312-13, *supra*, n. 7.

53. John W. Young to Brigham Young, May 9, 1866, Church Archives, *supra*, chap. 1, n. 2.

54. Preston Nibley, *Brigham Young, The Man and His Work*, 7th ed. (Salt Lake City: Deseret Book Co., 1974), pp. 447-48.

55. Milliken, Beginnings of Mormonism, 5:42, *supra*, n. 39.

56. *Auburn Daily Bulletin*, August 31, 1877.

57. *Ontario Republican Times*, 1857 clippings otherwise undated, in Church Archives, *supra*, chap. 1, n. 2.

58. Gates, *Life Story of Brigham Young*, pp. 19-20, *supra*, n. 12.

59. HBY, 25:438, *supra*, chap. 1, n. 3.

60. Allen, "Brigham Young and Mormonism," pp. 5-6, *supra*, n. 42.

## Chapter 4

1. Of the three brothers who were Methodist ministers before their conversions to the Mormon church, Joseph ultimately became, in 1835, the senior president of the LDS church's First Quorum of Seventy. See Joseph Smith, Jr., *History of the Church of Jesus Christ of Latter-day Saints*, 2nd ed., rev., 9 vols. (Salt Lake City: LDS Church, 1948), 2:181, 201-3.

2. HBY, 25:423, *supra*, chap. 1, n. 3.

3. Brigham Young, discourse of August 15, 1852, in *JD*, 6:290, *supra*, chap. 1, n. 4.

4. Brigham Young, address of July 11, 1852, ibid., 1:41.

5. Little, "Historical Items about Brigham Young," 2:6, *supra*, chap. 1, n. 2.

6. Brigham Young, remarks of April 6, 1860, in *JD*, 8:37, *supra*, chap. 1, n. 4.

7. Brigham Young, discourse of June 3, 1871, ibid., 14:197. Brigham spoke in a similar vein on another occasion: "I did not believe in the sectarian religion, I could not see any utility in it, any further than a moral character was concerned, yet I believed the Bible." *JD*, 4:104, *supra*, chap. 1, n. 4.

8. HBY, 25:423, *supra*, chap. 1, n. 3.

9. Brigham Young, remarks of April 6, 1860, in *JD*, 8:37-38, *supra*, chap. 1, n. 4.

10. Ora H. Barlow, "Family Recordings of Nauvoo," Church Archives, *supra*, chap. 1, n. 2. For another, similar account, see HBY, 25:423, *supra*, chap. 1, n. 3.

11. Brigham Young, remarks of October 6, 1870, in *JD*, 13:267, *supra*, chap. 1, n. 4.

12. Brigham Young, remarks of August 27, 1871, ibid., 14:244-24.

13. Little, "Biography of Lorenzo Dow Young," p. 29, *supra*, chap. 1, n. 15.

14. HBY, 25:326, *supra*, chap. 1., n. 3.

15. Ibid., 25:326-27. The account reads: "About that time [1824] I received license to speak in public."

16. Franklin Wheeler Young, "Notes on the Young Family," p. 10, Church Archives, *supra*, chap. 1, n. 2.

17. HBY, 25:423, *supra*, chap. 1, n. 3. In another account, Brigham stated he was twenty-three. A Methodist community was organized in Auburn in 1819 and Brigham probably attended services there. Unfortunately, his membership cannot be verified as the records were subsequently destroyed by fire.

18. Ibid., 25:311. The only mention of Joseph's having become a Methodist minister is the statement of Brigham Young that Joseph "was a Methodist preacher for many years." Perhaps the first of John Young, Sr.'s

children to make a full commitment to Christ was Rhoda, who married Methodist minister John P. Greene in 1813.

19. Ibid., 25:407.

20. Ibid., 25:327.

21. Little, "Historical Items about Brigham Young," 2:2, *supra,* chap. 1, n. 2.

22. HBY, 25:327, *supra,* chap. 1, n. 3.

23. Ibid.

24. Ibid.

## Chapter 5

1. See Joseph Smith, *History of the Church,* 1:18, *supra,* chap. 4, n. 1.; Heber C. Kimball, account in *Deseret News,* March 31, 1858; and Barlow, *Family Recordings of Nauvoo,* p. 29, *supra,* chap. 4, n. 10. The count of eight members of the John Young, Sr. family includes Heber C. Kimball's wife Vilate, who was Suzannah's daughter, John P. Greene, and Heber C. Kimball.

2. Barlow, "Family Recordings of Nauvoo," p. 29, *supra,* chap. 4, n. 10.

3. Kimball, *Deseret News, supra,* n. 1.

4. Hayden, *Syracuse Sunday Herald, supra,* chap. 3, n. 7.

5. HBY, 25:360, *supra,* chap. 1, n. 3.

6. Brigham Young, discourse of April 6, 1855, in *JD,* 2:249, *supra,* chap. 1, n. 4; and HBY, 25:424, *supra,* chap. 1, n. 3.

7. HBY, 25:361, *supra,* chap. 1, n. 3. Apparently the proprietor of Tomlinson's Inn was also favorably impressed by the book, either at the time of Samuel Smith's visit or later. See the 1832 list of members of the Mendon Branch on page 69 of this volume.

8. Ibid.

9. Brigham once stated: "The next spring [1830] I first saw the Book of Mormon, which brother Samuel H. Smith brought and left with my brother Phinehas H. Young." Ibid., 25:424.

10. Lucy Mack Smith, *History of Joseph Smith, supra,* chap. 3, n. 31.

11. Ibid., p. 170.

12. HBY, 25:361, *supra,* chap. 1, n. 3.

13. Brigham Young, discourse of August 8, 1852, in *JD,* 3:91, *supra,* chap. 1, n. 4.

14. HBY, 25:424, *supra,* chap. 1, n. 3.

15. Eunice E. Curtis, *The Ancestors and Descendants of Enos Curtis and Ruth Franklin—Utah Pioneers, 1783-1964, and Related Families* (Salt Lake City, n. p., n. d.), p. 13.

16. HBY, 25:374, *supra*, chap 1, n. 3. See Solomon Chamberlain, "A Short Sketch of the Life of Solomon Chamberlain," MS in the possession of Mrs. Albert D. Swensen, Provo, Utah, also reproduced in Larry C. Porter, "A Study of the Origins of the Church of Jesus Christ of Latter-day Saints in the States of New York and Pennsylvania, 1816-1831" (Ph.D. Dissertation, Brigham Young University, 1971), pp. 360-64.

17. Ibid.

18. Ibid., 25:374-75

19. Ibid., 25:375.

20. Ibid.

21. Kimball, *Deseret News*, *supra*, n. 1.

22. HBY, 25:424, *supra*, chap. 1., n. 3.

23. Ibid.

24. Ibid., 25:376.

25. Ibid.

26. Ibid., 25:438.

27. See branch records noting that John, Sr.'s second wife, Hannah, and their son, Edward, were also baptized in 1832. See also Brigham Young, discourse of March 15, 1857, in *JD*, 4:281, *supra*, chap. 1, n. 4.

28. Ibid.

29. HBY, 25:438, *supra*, chap. 1, n. 3.

30. Ibid., 25:406.

31. Ibid., 25:310.

32. Mendon Branch records, Church Archives, *supra*, chap. 1, n. 2.

33. Heber C. Kimball, remarks of December 20, 1857, in *JD*, 6:132, *supra*, chap. 1, n. 4.

34. Orson F. Whitney, *Life of Heber C. Kimball*, 4th ed. (Salt Lake City: Bookcraft, 1974), p. 19.

35. By 1832 the new church had already met with considerable hostility in New York, Pennsylvania, and Ohio. the principal leaders and most of their followers vacated New York in 1831, in large measure owing to hostilities that had commenced soon after the church was organized. By the time Brigham Young was baptized, Joseph Smith had been arrested twice (in New York) and tarred and feathered once (in Ohio). See Smith, *History of the Church*, 1: 88-98, 262-65, *supra*, chap. 4, n. 1.

36. *Wayne Sentinel* (Palmyra, N.Y.), April 18, 1832.

37. Historical Sketch of the Baptist Church of Mendon, Monroe County, New York, in *Minutes of the 27th Anniversary of the Monroe Baptist Association, October 5-6, 1864* (Rochester, N.Y., 1864), p. 18.

38. Hiram K. Stimson, *From the Stagecoach to the Pulpit* (St. Louis, 1874), p. 92.

39. Historical Sketch, p. 18, *supra*, n. 37.

40. Brigham Young, discourse of June 28, 1873, in *JD*, 16:67, *supra*, *chap. 1, n. 4.*

41. *Ontario Republican Times*, *supra*, chap. 3, n. 57.

42. *Ontario Republican Times*, August 27, 1857.

43. The account continues: "After I had joined the Church, I became somewhat accustomed to public speaking. Once in passing through No. 9 I stopped and preached in the schoolhouse north of Mr. Mack's." Ibid., July 23, 1858.

## Chapter 6

1. Brigham Young, discourse of March 14, 1857, in *JD*, 4:28, *supra*, chap. 1, n. 4.

2. HBY, 25:438, *supra*, chap. 1, n. 3.

3. Ibid., 25:439; and *Ontario Republican Times*, July 23, 1858.

4. Brigham Young, discourse of August 17, 1856, in *JD*, 4:20-21, *supra*, chap. 1, n. 4. See also *Ontario Republican Times*, July 23, 1858.

5. Brigham Young, discourse of February 29, 1863, in *JD*, 1:313-14, *supra*, chap. 1, n. 4.

6. Brigham Young, discourse of August 31, 1856, ibid., 4:34-35.

7. HBY, 25:439, *supra*, chap. 1, n. 3.

8. Ibid.

9. Joseph Young to Lewis Harvey, November 16, 1880, Special Collections, Harold B. Lee Library, Brigham Young University, Provo, Utah.

10. HBY, 25:439, *supra*, chap. 1, n. 3.

11. Ibid.

12. Ibid., 25:440.

13. See ibid., 25:295; Monroe County Deeds, Liber 28, p. 23, *supra*, chap. 3, n. 32; and John Young Revolutionary War Pension File, *supra*, chap. 1, n. 28.

14. Little, "Biography of Lorenzo Dow Young," p. 42, *supra*, chap. 1, n. 15.

15. Brigham Young, discourse of February 3, 1867, in *JD*, 11:295-96, *supra*, chap. 1, n. 4.

16. See Joseph Smith, *History of the Church*, 2:187, *supra*, chap. 4, n. 1. See also Doctrine and Covenants 107:23.

17. HBY, 25:472, *supra*, chap. 1, n. 3.

65491

18. Ibid., 25:487.

19. Ibid.

20. Ibid., 25:503-4.

21. Doctrine and Covenants 118:4-5.

22. HBY, 25:646, *supra*, chap. 1, n. 3. For another account of Brigham's departure, see Roberts, *Comprehensive History*, 2:22-24, *supra*, chap. 1, n. 1.

23. Brigham Young, discourse of August 31, 1856, in *JD*, 4:34, *supra*, chap. 1, n. 4.

24. HBY, 25:664, *supra*, chap. 1, n. 3.

25. Ibid. For another, somewhat different account, see Joseph Smith, *History of the Church*, 4:24, *supra*, chap. 4, n.1.

26. HBY, 25:664, *supra*, chap. 1, n. 3. The Moravia Branch had evolved chiefly through the proselyting efforts of Elder Pelatiah Brown in the winter of 1838. Isaac C. Haight and his wife, the former Eliza Ann Snider, were "buried in the waters of baptism" on March 3, 1839, "much to the mortification of our friends." Journal of Isaac C. Haight, 1842-1850, Church Archives, *supra*, chap. 1, n. 2.

27. "Incidents in the Life of Mary Helen Grant," *History of the Reorganized Church of Jesus Christ of Latter Day Saints*, 10 (April 1917): 171.

28. HBY, 25:678-79, *supra*, chap. 1, n. 3.

29. Ibid., 25:679.

30. Ibid.

31. Nibley, *Brigham Young*, p. 31, *supra*, chap. 3, n. 54.

32. Brigham Young, discourse of August 31, 1856, in *JD*, 4:35-36, *supra*, chap. 1, n. 4. See also Roberts, *Comprehensive History*, 2:85-87, *supra*, chap. 1, n. 1; and Elden Jay Watson, ed., *Manuscript History of Brigham Young, 1801-1844* (Salt Lake City: privately published, 1968), p. 105. Brigham was appointed as president of the Quorum of the Twelve—which was to be the vital step to the presidency of the LDS church from that point forward—on January 19, 1841, while he and the Twelve were still in England. See Doctrine and Covenants 124:127.

# Index

*This book designed by*
*Bailey-Montague & Associates*

*Editorial work by*
*Howard A. Christy*

*Typesetting by*
*Eden Hill Publishing*

*Printing and binding by*
*Community Press*